6-6-67

The
CHURCH in the
RACIALLY
CHANGING
COMMUNITY

Prepared and edited by

Research and Survey
National Division
The Board of Missions of The Methodist Church

and published by

ABINGDON PRESS
New York   Nashville

The
CHURCH in the
RACIALLY
CHANGING
COMMUNITY

Robert L. WILSON and James H. DAVIS

METHODIST CHURCH

DEPT. OF RESEARCH AND SURVEY

THE CHURCH IN THE RACIALLY CHANGING COMMUNITY

Copyright © 1966 by Abingdon Press

Library of Congress Catalog Card Number: 66-11060

SET UP, PRINTED, AND BOUND BY THE
PARTHENON PRESS, AT NASHVILLE,
TENNESSEE, UNITED STATES OF AMERICA

1398949

To Murray H. Leiffer

UNDER WHOSE GUIDANCE WE DEVELOPED
OUR INTEREST IN RELIGIOUS RESEARCH

CONTENTS

The
CHURCH in the
RACIALLY
CHANGING
COMMUNITY

INTRODUCTION

Phoenix Heights is a type of neighborhood to be found in almost every American city. The large trees, well-kept lawns, and comfortable-looking houses, give the impression of a good place in which to live. The community began to develop shortly before World War I; the large number of two-story square houses reflect the type of dwelling popular in the 1920's.

Changes are taking place in the community, or, to be more specific, one major change. The number

11

of "For Sale" signs in evidence far exceeds the normal rate of property turnover. The easiest way to discover what is happening is to go by the elementary school during recess. A large number of Negro youngsters can be seen. A year ago all residents were white; today approximately 30 percent are Negro. Every new family who moves into the community is Negro.

Phoenix Heights Methodist Church has been one of the prominent community institutions for well over half a century. The large stone structure is located at an intersection near the geographical center of the neighborhood. The sanctuary was erected in 1912, and the educational wing was added in 1926. Over the years the congregation has maintained its building well. However, no major improvements have been undertaken for more than two years. The painting of several church school classrooms has been delayed, and the replacement of the boiler has been postponed pending a decision regarding the congregation's future.

At its peak Phoenix Heights Church was a strong congregation. However, the membership has steadily declined in recent years. Almost one member in ten no longer lives within commuting distance, while almost one in three resides outside the immediate neighborhood.

The church school has declined faster than the church membership. The loss has been particularly

12

noticeable in the children's division. A number of the younger families have purchased new homes in the suburban developments being erected on the edge of the city some seven to nine miles from Phoenix Heights.

Although the majority of the members still reside in the community, many of the leaders have moved out. These persons still come back to church. The increasing number of commuting members has been a matter of concern to the pastor, and he views with some apprehension the possible formation of a new congregation in a subdivision where several of his more active families now reside. While the trend to the suburbs has been going on for some time, the racial change taking place has speeded up the movement. The congregation had the greatest loss in membership in its history during the past year.

Surprisingly enough, and to the great relief of the official board, the church's income has held up rather well. By delaying any major building improvements the congregation was able to meet its asking for missions, pay all bills, and even provide a modest raise in salary for the pastor.

Within recent months the major topic of conversation among the church members has been the number of Negro families moving into the neighborhood. The members talk not only about their personal plans, whether to stay or move and when to do so, but what their church ought to do.

Among several of the board members there have

been discussions (but not in a board meeting) about what should be the strategy if "they should come to our church." As of now, no Negro has come. Some members feel, and are quite vocal in their opinions, that the attendance of a Negro at a worship service would result in the exodus of a sufficient number of the present members to threaten the church's existence. Other members do not share this opinion, but do not see how the new residents could support a church with a building as large as Phoenix Heights.

Several persons feel quite strongly that the church ought to relocate, preferably in an area near where they now live. It has been rumored that a Negro congregation is considering making an offer on the property. Many of the members, particularly the older persons who have lived in the neighborhood a long time, just can't bear the thought of selling their church. The insecurity about the future has been hard on congregational morale. Homecoming this year didn't have the usual crowd or spirit.

In the meantime, the ushers have been instructed by the pastor that if any Negro comes to worship, he is to be seated. However, the usual Race Relations Sunday pulpit exchange with a Negro pastor whose church is located close to downtown was omitted this year lest "it be misinterpreted."

The man most troubled by the change in the community is the pastor. A sincere, capable, energetic man in his mid-forties, he is in his second year of service at Phoenix Heights. His appointment to the

14

church was not as great a promotion as he had thought it was to be. The congregation was reputed to be considerably stronger than he found it.

The minister is beset by many questions. Can he work to evangelize the newcomers in the community? Dare he invite them to church? Would he be an adequate pastor to Negroes, having known only a few personally and those during his student days? Would there be a mass exodus of white members should Negroes come to worship? Would the financial program of the church collapse? What would be the attitude of his bishop if he offended his board by seeking Negro members? Should he take some drastic action now or hold on for another year and quietly move to another church?

The Phoenix Heights Methodist Church of the past generation is rapidly passing from the scene. What will be its future? More important, what will be the future of the Phoenix Heights community and what role will the church play in that future?

In practically every major city in America there is a community similar to Phoenix Heights. During the 1950's, the Negro population in cities of 50,000 and over increased by more than 50 percent. During the same period, the white residents of these cities increased by less than 5 percent. Many urban neighborhoods which were predominately Caucasian a decade ago are now Negro.

More than 4,500,000 Negroes were living in the 10 largest cities at the time of the 1960 United States

Census. This number represents almost one out of four Negroes in the United States. And the Negro migration to the cities—large and small—is continuing.

Protestant churches in every large city are facing an uncertain future in racially changing communities. The purpose of this book is to aid such churches. An attempt will be made to show what happens to and within a congregation when the church is located in a community that is changing from Caucasian to Negro. The different responses of churches and the results of their varied courses of action will be described. It is hoped that this study will give some guidance to leaders in both the local churches and the denomination as they face the necessity of making decisions regarding churches in communities of racial change.

The material in this report is based on studies of more than sixty churches located in twenty-two cities. Included are seven of the ten largest cities in the country, eight of the next forty largest cities selected on a random basis, and seven additional cities, with a 1960 population of 100,000 or more, chosen because of the presence of churches in racially changing communities. The cities, located in all sections of the country, provide a cross section of urban America.

The churches selected for study are those which are located in a community which is changing from white to Negro, or which has recently completed such a transition. Included among the more than

16

sixty churches studied are practically all types of urban congregations. These range from a church which, at its height, had the largest membership in the annual conference, to a small neighborhood church which had never had more than 150 members. In those cases where a Methodist congregation had sold its building during the past decade, the current use of the old church property was studied.

The churches in this study are located in areas which, up to the time of racial change, were stable residential neighborhoods. Most of the communities were developed during the 1920's, although a few originated prior to World War I. In several instances the neighborhood had been built in the late 1940's immediately following World War II. Two churches in this study are located along what had been the city's outer line of defense and the scene of a battle during the Civil War.

Data upon which this report is based came from a variety of sources. The Research and Survey files of the National Division of the Board of Missions and of the research departments of the seminaries provided valuable historical data. The researchers were given access to a variety of helpful records, particularly the files of several district superintendents and local churches.

The major sources of data were interviews conducted by the Research and Survey staff in the racially changing communities. Persons interviewed included the present and previous pastors of the churches in the study, and white and Negro lay members of these churches. The district superintendents and annual conference executives provided valuable insights into the local situation. Detailed statistical data were provided by some of the congregations in the study.

Interviews were sought with persons who could provide information on what was happening in the racially changing communities. Many informal interviews were held with businessmen, school administrators, teachers, and persons in the city government.

The names of the churches in this study and the cities in which they are located are not included in this report. Churches described in detail have been given fictitious names. By omitting actual names, the study cannot be replicated at some future date. Because of the nature of the subject, it was deemed necessary to protect the anonymity of the persons interviewed and the churches studied. Much of the data on which this report is based could not have been secured if the persons interviewed had not been assured of anonymity. The presentation of the material is more forthright than it could have been if people and places were identified.

This report has been made possible because scores of Methodists were willing to share their firsthand experiences of what happened when their churches and homes were in racially changing communities. All who profit from this report will owe these persons a debt of gratitude.

18

I

WHEN THE NEIGHBORHOOD CHANGES

Almost half of the houses along two blocks of a treelined street had red and white realtor "For Sale" signs on the small front lawns. Many of the signs were already labeled "Sold." The community was in the midst of its most drastic upheaval since the homes were constructed on the prairie almost thirty years ago. Up to this time the neighborhood had been a stable residential community, one of the most desirable places in the city in which to live.

North of the two blocks where the "For Sale"

signs were located, almost all of the inhabitants were Negro. All of the persons living south of this area were white. The two-block strip was the growing edge of the city's vast Negro ghetto. The neighborhood was in the process of changing from one in which all of the residents were white to one where the vast majority of the inhabitants would be Negro.

No aspect of community life remains unaffected when an area changes from white to Negro. A new group of people move into the old neighborhood. Some local institutions may not survive the changes; others will make drastic adaptations and become a part of the new community. This chapter will describe what happens when the neighborhood changes from white to Negro.

People Must Go Somewhere

To understand the need for the expansion of the Negro communities in the large cities, it is necessary to be aware of the extent of Negro migration. For many years Negro people have been moving from the South to the North and West. They have been moving from rural areas in the South to the urban centers in the South and in the North and West.

The extent of this migration can be seen by comparing the proportion of Negroes living in the eleven states which made up the Confederacy with the corresponding figure of one or two decades ago. In

1940, 69.0 percent of the Negroes lived in the former Confederate States. By 1950 this proportion had dropped to 60.2 percent and by 1960 it was 52.2 percent. Thus almost one half of the Negroes in the United States live outside the Old South.

Another way of looking at this migration is to compare the percentage of increase in the Negro population within the former Confederate States with the percentage of increase of the Negro population in the rest of the country. In the ten-year period 1950-60 the Negro population in the southern states increased 8.9 percent; in the rest of the country the Negro population increased 50.2 percent. For the country as a whole the increase in the Negro population was 25.4 percent.

Negroes who leave the rural areas of the South move to the city. Some may move to a city nearby, others move to cities in the North and West. Negroes who live outside of the South tend to be found in the central city of a large metropolitan area. In 1960 more than four and a half million Negroes lived within the corporate limits of fifteen large cities[1] outside the South. This number represents slightly more than one out of four (25.2 percent) of all of the Negroes in the United States.

In 1948 the United States Supreme Court ruled that restrictive covenants were legally unenforceable.

---

[1] Baltimore, Boston, Buffalo, Chicago, Cincinnati, Cleveland, Denver, Detroit, Los Angeles, New York, Philadelphia, Pittsburgh, San Francisco, Seattle, Washington, D.C.

Negroes could no longer be prevented from purchasing homes in previously all-white neighborhoods. This decision coincided with increasing Negro prosperity and large-scale migration to the city. Negroes began to move from the overcrowded dilapidated sections into the nearby better houses and neighborhoods. The racially changing community became a problem in some part of every major city.

The Negro residents of large urban centers are likely to be concentrated in the predominately Negro section of the central city. These Negro communities have increased by expanding into adjacent white neighborhoods. Neighborhoods tend to be either all white, all Negro, or in the process of changing from white to Negro. A study of the trend in the decade 1940-50 demonstrated that residential segregation increased during this period.[2] There are indications that this trend continues to hold true. While today more Negroes living in the metropolitan areas are located outside the central city, many still reside in predominately Negro enclaves. Many suburban communities are experiencing the development of large Negro sections. In one area included in this study there is every indication that a suburban municipality will become entirely Negro.

The newest arrival in the city begins at the bottom of the social and economic ladder. As the latest to come he inherits the least desirable part of town, the

[2] Donald O. Cowgill, "Trends in Residential Segregation of Non-whites," *American Sociological Review* February, 1955, p. 47.

section which is being abandoned by members of an earlier group who are making their place in the larger society. The newest immigrant receives not only the hand-me-down house and neighborhood, he also receives hand-me-down institutions. In one city a Methodist church began as a white English-speaking congregation, continued as an Italian-speaking group, and was passed on to a Spanish-speaking one.

Unlike the European immigrant the Negro cannot lose his minority status and become a part of the larger society. The Negro's high degree of conspicuousness makes him readily identifiable as a Negro. Thus, unlike the Norwegian, Italian, or Mexican, he cannot in a generation lose the distinctive social characteristics which set him apart from the larger society. The European background of the Polish immigrant's son may be known only by the spelling of his name. If he so desires he can change his name. The Negro continues to be identified as a Negro.

The result has been a resistance to the Negroes moving into white neighborhoods. Every large city has its history of violent incidents as attempts have been made to prevent the growth of the Negro community into a particular area. Nevertheless, Negroes continue to migrate to the city. One city would be nine times its present population if its overall density were as high as that of its Negro section. The ghetto, already an area of high population density, has to expand. It does so by pushing outward into adjacent white neighborhoods. Even the Negro increase in sub-

23

urban communities is generally an expansion of old and small Negro neighborhoods.

Continuing Change

"I don't really mind the Colored moving in too much, but I hate to see the neighborhood become a slum." This was the comment of a housewife who was an active church member and an officer in the Woman's Society. To any thinking person it is obvious that the race of the residents is not responsible for the deterioration of the neighborhood. But some communities in the process of being passed on from one group to another do become slums.

The neighborhood which changes racially does not become static. The continued immigration of Negro people to the large cities exerts tremendous pressure on the available housing. The growing pressure of population forces the Negro community to expand and change as the middle-class Negro families move farther out. They are replaced by persons not as well educated, the less affluent, and newer arrivals in the city. The community then tends to deteriorate. The schools, already overcrowded, get worse. Street safety becomes a continuing problem. Liquor stores and taverns multiply. Newspapers write shocking articles on the horrible conditions in the area. Store-front churches occupy buildings that were once thriving neighborhood businesses. The large well-established Negro congregations which purchased their buildings from the original white congregations find that their members have moved out of the area and are commuting back to the church.

Eight years ago one community began its first period of racial change. At the time there were two types of signs prominently displayed on many of the houses. One was a typical red and white real estate broker's "For Sale" sign. The other type of sign was green and yellow with the words, "Not for Sale —I believe in my neighbor and my community." Within eighteen months neither the "For Sale" nor the "Not for Sale" signs were in evidence. The efforts to stabilize the community had failed, and practically all of the white residents had moved away. For a couple of years the neighborhood settled down as a quiet residential area, much the same as it had been when the population was predominately white. Then it began to change again. An urban renewal project close to the center of the city forced many families to relocate. Many moved into the section. The original Negro purchasers relocated farther out. The illegal subdividing of houses into apartments increased to meet the housing needs. The evidence of deterioration became obvious. Now, eight years after the first neighborhood change, the community can be classified as a slum. A Negro congregation of one of the old-line denominations, which purchased its building from a white group of the same denomination, is considering moving out of the area. It is unsuccessful in ministering to the type of person who now lives there.

25

Profit from Panic

Two conditions help make it possible for persons to take advantage of the panic of white residents in a racially changing community. The first is the desperate need for housing for Negroes, which provides a ready market for any available property. The second is the urgency with which the white residents want to leave the changing neighborhood, making them willing to sell for a low price. The situation is ideal for the speculator who buys homes from the fleeing whites at a low figure and immediately resells them to Negroes at a considerable profit.

It is to some persons' advantage to encourage panic-selling. The real estate brokers' commissions on the sale of practically every house in a neighborhood can total up to a considerable amount. The white residents are frequently subjected to a barrage of advertisements designed to capitalize on their fear of being left in a Negro community and unable to sell their houses. One community was flooded with flyers stating, "We have a buyer for your house." These advertisements were issued at regular intervals. On the back were listed the properties sold since the previous leaflet. Some advertisements are less subtle, as the postcard which read, "Let us sell your house before it is too late."

Other techniques to create panic-selling have been reported. One example is the sending of two salesmen, one white and one Negro, to the same block.

While the Negro salesman knocks on doors on one side of the street, the white salesman does so on the other. He points out to the owners that their neighbors are going to sell their homes to Negroes, using the Negro salesman as tangible evidence. Another reported technique is the hiring of a Negro lady with several children to walk around in the neighborhood. This is taken as evidence by the residents that Negroes have moved into the neighborhood or at least into a community nearby. A high price may be paid to the first white owner who sells to a Negro family. After the first Negroes have moved in they are cited as evidence of the trend, and the price offered to subsequent white sellers is much lower.

Considerable profit is made by those who purchase houses from the fleeing white residents and resell them to Negroes. Nonresident speculators purchase property in racially changing communities by securing a conventional mortgage. They then resell the property to Negroes on an installment contract basis at a large profit. A study of property transactions in one neighborhood revealed that when the inhabitants were white, none of the properties were held on an installment contract basis. After the racial change approximately six out of seven properties were being purchased on an installment contract basis.[3]

The installment contract works to the advantage of the seller. It is easy to inflate the price because

---

[3] *Selling and Buying Real Estate in a Racially Changing Neighborhood* (Chicago Commission on Human Relations, 1962), p. 9.

the purchaser does not get the kind of counsel associated with securing a mortgage. The installment contract does not have the safeguards of the mortgage or the foreclosure proceedings. The purchaser does not build up equity in the property and can easily lose all his investment should he be unable to continue the payments.

A study of the price paid by the speculator and the resale price to the Negro buyer on the installment contract gives some indication of the extent of the profit: "The percentage increase in price ranged from a low of 35 percent to a high of 115 percent. The average increase in price between what the nonresident speculator paid and the price on the resale installment contract was 73 percent." [4]

Two specific cases will illustrate the type of profit which can be made in racially changing communities. A two-story frame house was purchased from the white owner by a nonresident speculator for $9,500. This person secured a mortgage for $9,000 on which the payments were $78.50 per month. The house was then sold to a Negro purchaser on an installment contract basis for $18,300. The Negro's down payment was $1,500 and his monthly payments $150.[5]

In another case a nonresident speculator purchased a two-story frame house from a white owner for $10,000. He made a payment of $3,000 and secured a conventional mortgage for the balance of $7,000.

[4] *Ibid.*, p. 5.
[5] *Ibid.*, p. 33.

The monthly payments were $79. The dwelling was then sold to a Negro buyer on an installment contract for $17,900. The down payment was $1,500 and the monthly payments were $135. It is easy to see why some persons encourage panic-selling.[6]

The Negro buyer like the white seller is a victim. The Negro has only the choice of remaining in the overcrowded substandard housing in the ghetto or braving white hostility and paying an exorbitant price for a house. For parents with the normal amount of concern and ambition for their children the choice is obvious. No price is too high to escape from the slums.

The cost of a house to a Negro purchaser contributes to the deterioration of the property and neighborhood. Because of the high monthly payments the family has little money available for maintenance of the property. Furthermore the houses are at an age when they generally need major repairs. Because these repairs cannot be made the property becomes run-down. To meet expenses some families find it necessary to rent a room or two. This causes overcrowding and speeds the process of deterioration.

Pressure on the Public School

One of the neighborhood institutions most drastically affected by a period of racial change is the public school. The incoming Negro population tends

[6] *Ibid.,* p. 34.

to be younger than the group moving out. The incoming group has many young families. The birth rate is high. The result is a large increase in the number of children who must be cared for by the public school. The public schools in the community generally do not have enough classroom facilities for the increased number of children. The result is extensive use of mobile classrooms or the necessity for the school to go on double sessions.

The increase in numbers is not the only problem which a school administrator must face. Community tensions come to focus in the school. Adequate educational standards are hard to maintain during a time of rapid change. It is difficult to secure and retain a teaching staff. Many teachers transfer from schools in racially changing communities to those located in less difficult places.

The schools' problems are illustrated by the comments of a principal whose school is located in a community which has practically completed the change from white to Negro. The principal, a middle-aged lady, had been in charge of this school for seventeen years. During the course of racial change the enrollment increased from 906 white pupils to 1,274 pupils, of whom less than 50 were white. In one academic year 639 students transferred in and 356 transferred out. The principal reported that an increase of only 28 more pupils would mean that the school would have to be operated on double sessions. She also said that she had a high rate of teacher transfer—22 at the end of the year in which the racial change took place, primarily because of disciplinary problems.

The principal talked of the difficulty she had in maintaining adequate educational standards in a transitional period. She commented on the educational background of some of her pupils, saying, "They are the product of America's neglect." Her superintendent had offered her a different school. So far she had refused, but confessed that she did not know how long she could take the strain of her present assignment.

In another neighborhood which has completed the racial change, 23.6 percent of the population is of elementary school age. In that city only 16.2 percent of the entire population is in this age group.

The same community is served by 28 elementary schools and 3 upper grade centers with a total of more than 44,000 students. By overcrowding the classrooms to accommodate an average of 40 students per classroom in all operating schools in the area—with the exception of two schools with only 20 pupils per class—and by using 58 mobile classrooms, the total enrollment has been accommodated without resorting to double shifts.

In this community 14 new schools have been constructed within the past five years. Within the past seven years more than 17 million dollars were invested in school capital improvement, of which 11 million dollars were put into school construction.

31

Despite these efforts classrooms must accommodate an average of 40 students.[7]

The Effect on Business

Businesses located in a racially changing neighborhood will be drastically affected by the population movement. Businessmen like the rest of the community will move their residences out of the neighborhood, even though some will continue to commute back to their places of business.

Some businesses will adapt and survive in the new neighborhood. Those which can secure customers from the incoming group to replace those they are losing from the outgoing residents can remain. Even though the new population may be greater than the former, families may be larger, income lower, and purchasing power greatly reduced. With a lower purchasing power fewer stores can be supported. The result is fewer business establishments with a smaller variety of merchandise available to the residents. Stores which survive tend to be those which handle convenience goods such as food and other necessities. Other stores may survive by making available small loans and selling on credit.

In one community the block-long neighborhood business district was in the process of transition. There were two vacant stores, and it was reported that several others were making plans to relocate when

[7] *Lawndale: . . . Background for Planning,* Part 1 (Chicago Community Renewal Program), p. 14.

their leases expired. In this particular section a major problem for the small store owners was raids by teen-age gangs of Negro boys. The technique is for a gang of eight to twelve boys to rush into the store, pick up any items they wish, and leave. The shop owner is helpless to prevent this attack. A jewelry store and a grocery store have recently been subjected to such a raid.

Persons with professional offices in a racially changing community are faced with the problem of relocating or attempting to stay. In either case they have to develop a new clientele either from among the new population in the neighborhood where the office is located or from among the residents of the community into which they move. Some professional persons operate two offices for a time but close the first office after getting established in the new location.

Some insights into the nature of business activity in a racially changing community are given by a study of one area which changed between 1954 and 1958.[8] During this period the total business activity decreased. However, the number of eating and drinking places increased by approximately 20 percent. The number of liquor stores located in the area grew by 17 percent.

A business, like other community institutions, loses its neighborhood clientele in the process of racial

[8] *Ibid.,* p. 33.

changes. It must adapt to the neighborhood and win a new group of customers if it is going to survive. The only alternative is to close and seek a new location in some other community.

The Problem of Policing

For the police officer an area undergoing racial change is a less desirable assignment. Officers with seniority find it advantageous to request a transfer to some other district. Men with less training and experience may be assigned to such areas. The citizens may lose their confidence in the police.

In one city a church was carrying on a rather extensive youth program. The church leaders worked out an informal agreement with the police officers in an adjoining district. If it were necessary to summon the police, officers from that district would respond, although it meant they would be traveling several blocks out of their own territory. The churchmen felt that they would receive better service from the police stationed in the more stable residential community.

An increase in crime may come with the period of transition. While the neighborhood may be patrolled by the same number or even an increased number of police officers, the increase in crime will leave people with the feeling that the area is inadequately policed. Furthermore, a neighborhood in transition is fertile ground for rumors, so that minor incidents may take on major proportions. While crime may increase during the disorganized period of transition, the neighborhood may tend to settle down after the change is complete. The feeling that the area is unsafe is a prime reason for the eagerness of many white residents to leave.

Options for the Church 1398949

The church, like other institutions, is greatly influenced by what takes place in the neighborhood. The church, however, has a membership with a high degree of loyalty which enables it to react slowly to the changing community.

The church which finds itself in an area of racial transition has three options. It can sell the building and relocate in some other part of the city. It can attempt to remain a white congregation using its present facilities, depending upon a membership which commutes back to the church. Or it can attempt to minister to whoever moves into the community.

Churches have followed each of these courses of action. The following chapters will describe in detail the ways congregations have responded to racially changing communities.

II

CHURCH MEMBERS ARE PEOPLE TOO

The title of a three-page mimeographed leaflet left in the mailboxes of all houses in a seven-block area read, "Does property value go down because of Negroes, neglect, or panic?" The leaflet went on to announce a meeting the following Tuesday evening, the purpose of which was to organize in order to "minimize panic-selling." Questions to be discussed by a panel included, "What makes property values go down? Why do 'they' say whites will no longer buy?" The statement concluded, "We live in one of the most pleasant and convenient sections of the city; why not work a little to keep it that way? Come to the meeting Tuesday evening. Meet and become better aquainted with your neighbors."

The community in which the leaflets were circulated is one in the beginning of racial change. A few Negro families have moved into the neighborhood. By and large the white residents do not want to leave; it is a convenient and pleasant area. Nevertheless, they are apprehensive about the future. The Negro community has been expanding. The group sponsoring the meeting is not dedicated to the exclusion of Negroes; one of the persons taking part in a panel is a Negro lady who lives in the neighborhood. They hope to prevent panic-selling and the collapse of the community. They want to remain, so they are trying to organize to maintain the community. However, the Negro population in the city is steadily increasing. It has to expand in some direction. In all probability, in a matter of time the neighborhood will have a majority of Negro residents. The citizens' organization may minimize the panic and help provide an orderly transition, but its chances of attaining a stable interracial community are not encouraging.

The individual living in the community described above has many roles. He may be a church member, a parent, a businessman, and a homeowner. His course of action in a given situation will be influenced by these various roles. The manner in which a person reacts in his role as a church member will be influenced by the way he views himself as a property owner or a businessman.

The racially changing community influences the individual in many ways. It may affect his business. It certainly will affect the value of his house—if not the actual selling price, at least the desirability of living in the house. The changing neighborhood may cause anxiety about the quality of education which his children are receiving.

This chapter will focus on some of the ways the lives of the church members are affected by the changes taking place in the communities around them.

The Homeowner

The largest purchase which the average family makes is a house. A considerable proportion of its income goes into mortgage payments for a period of twenty to thirty years. The investment is large enough to be a matter of concern when the family feels that the value of its property may drastically decrease.

The value of a house depends not only on the type and size of the structure but on the desirability of the community as a place to live. When a family buys a house, it is in effect selecting a community which it considers to be a good place to live. When for any reason the neighborhood is considered undesirable by a large portion of the population, the market for, and hence the value of, a particular property is reduced. A racially changing community is one into which a large proportion of the population will not move.

Furthermore, the techniques of blockbusting and induced panic-selling tend to provide a situation in which some individuals lose money on their property. During the period of transition the white family may be so anxious to leave that it sells the house at a lower figure than the property would normally be worth. A certain neighborhood had one Negro family which had been living there approximately six months. The Negro community was expanding in the direction of this community, so that it was apparent that more Negroes would be moving there in the near future. One white family, because the husband was transferred, was forced to put its house up for sale. The realtor who was consulted said that he could sell the home for approximately 10 percent less than the recent selling price of similar houses in the community. When the owner protested that his house ought to have a higher value, the real estate agent responded, "Yes, but one of 'them' has already moved into the community."

There is no question but that the fear of the home-owner is real and not without some justification. If he sells his house at its fair market value, he is selling an older dwelling while he may be moving into a new and higher-priced structure. Even if he manages to secure a house at the same price, he still has the costs of selling his old house and purchasing another, plus the expense of moving. In one eastern city it

39

was estimated that in selling a house for $12,000 and purchasing another for $12,000, the individual would pay a minimum of $1,342 in fees and settlement charges. The cost of moving his furnishings would be added to this amount.

Anyone can talk about his fear of losing money on the sale of his house without fear of disapproval by his friends and neighbors. Everyone feels he can understand the profit and loss aspects of a real estate transaction. The persons who complain about a dollar loss receive sympathy. While this loss can be real, it can also be a way of concealing other feelings. The person who says, "I, personally, would not object to having Negroes living in the neighborhood if it would not adversely affect the value of my house," may really mean that he does not want Negroes in the community. The expressed fear of decreased property value can be a socially acceptable method of expressing other unarticulated fears and prejudices. The individual may know that he should not have negative feelings toward Negroes, but he may have them nevertheless. By expressing these in terms of his concern over the value of his house, he may receive sympathy instead of condemnation.

The Parent

The individual caught in the racially changing community may be a parent. As such he has the normal concern for the welfare of his family. The kind of environment in which his children are to grow up is very important. This is particularly so for families with school-age children, especially those in junior and senior high school. Children in this age range are less in the protective atmosphere of the home than are younger children and take greater part in school and community activities.

The period of racial change is one of turmoil in certain community institutions, particularly in the school. A church may resist the change, but a school cannot do so. High educational standards are difficult to maintain while the white pupils are leaving and the Negro pupils are coming in. The problem is further compounded by a turnover of teachers. More young families are among the newcomers, so that there are more school-age children in the community than when it was a white neighborhood. The consequence of this may be an overcrowded school that is forced to use mobile classrooms or to go on double shifts. The conscientious parent views these developments and their possible effect on his child's education with justifiable apprehension.

The parent is concerned about the social group of which his child is a part. He realizes that the peer group exerts a strong influence. Families with teenagers are the most apprehensive. While probability of interracial marriage is very slight, many parents are haunted by this possibility and act accordingly. One pastor serving in a changing community reported how he had always endeavored to teach his

41

children the concepts of equality of all persons regardless of race. However, when his teen-age daughter walked home from school two days in a row with the same Negro boy, he took her aside and cautioned her against becoming too friendly.

The residents in a changing community are concerned about physical safety. This is particularly true on the part of parents. A neighborhood in the process of change tends to have a greater degree of disorganization than it had before the change, or than it will have after the change is complete. Tension may exist between white and Negro teen-agers. An argument between a white and a Negro youth which would go unnoticed in an ordinary neighborhood may be magnified into a major incident.

The fear of crime and violence probably is one of the main reasons why white families move out of racially changing communities. Every large city has its Negro area with a high crime rate. That the cause may not be related to race does not enter into the thinking of the white family which considers moving. All that it takes is for a house in the neighborhood to be looted, or for a purse-snatching to occur, to clearly demonstrate to the remaining white residents that they ought to leave as soon as possible. In many communities in transition there is just enough crime to provide a foundation for the rumors. Three of the parsonages of churches in this study were burglarized.

Typical is the comment of one layman who has

moved but still returns to the church of which he is an official:

I really didn't want to move. I had to pay almost $5,000 more for the place I bought than what I got for my house. Besides, I almost had my house paid for. I really couldn't afford to move, but I couldn't stay here either.

It was hard on the kids. John, my oldest boy, is sixteen. It got so they were afraid to go out at night. They used to go bowling and the whole gang would come to my place and I'd walk them home with the dog. One night five of them coming to our place after MYF were stopped and searched by the police. They had to put their hands on the top of the squad car while the cops searched them. I said that if the neighborhood has gotten so bad that the kids can't come home from MYF without that kind of thing, we were getting out. That's when we decided to move.

The Businessman

The small businessman whose customers are drawn from the neighborhood may experience real hardship as the community changes from white to Negro. If it is a business such as a grocery, which can serve Negro as well as white customers, the owner may survive by moving out of the neighborhood and commuting back to his store.

The population change has considerable influence upon local business. In one neighborhood the business activity declined during a four-year period of

43

racial change. Although the total population of the community increased, the family income was lower, which resulted in lower purchasing power. Some stores were forced to close.

In the case of a professional person or a business which is dependent on a long-cultivated clientele the results can be disastrous. The years of getting established in a neighborhood and of developing a good reputation will be lost as the community changes. Such a business or professional person has the choice of either relocating and facing the task of getting established in another area or of having to go through the process of developing a new clientele from among the new residents of the old community.

The Church Member

The individual who finds his home located in a racially changing community may be a church member. Over the years his church has consciously attempted to persuade him to accept certain values. The extent of the church's influence on the individual's decisions cannot be known. It is probably less than the pastor would like but more than many people assume.

An important factor for the pastor or denominational executive to keep in mind in consulting with local church leaders in a racially changing neighborhood is that the church members occupy many roles in the community. The decision regarding the policy of a local congregation is made not by persons who are church members only, but who are also parents, homeowners, businessmen, and so forth. Therefore, when the relocation of the church is considered, the businessman on the committee may think in terms of the factors that are forcing him to find a new location for his store.

A church member may find his convictions or the teaching of his church in conflict with the decisions he makes. As a Christian he may believe in the equality of all persons, but as a parent he does not wish to jeopardize the educational development of his children. The teachings about brotherhood may be in direct conflict with the fears which he has as a homeowner concerning the possible decrease in property value. The individual occupies many roles in the community and is a part of many groups. All of these may exert some influence on his specific course of action.

For a white family to remain in a racially changing community is to go against a number of strong influences favoring a move. As the proportion of Negro residents increases, the remaining whites become increasingly conscious of their minority status. Ultimately the vast majority manage to move. To do so may require financial sacrifice and considerable inconvenience. Most people are willing to pay the necessary price.

45

The only white persons who seem to remain in a community after Negroes constitute a large majority of the population are those who cannot leave. These tend to be elderly people who do not wish to leave their home or, more likely, cannot afford to relocate, who have been caught in a maelstrom of social forces over which they have no control. Plans to spend their retirement among friends and in the home on which they struggled for many years to make payments have been frustrated. In any changing community such persons can easily be seen—the elderly white gentleman working in his flower garden, or the lady with cane in hand carrying a small bag of groceries from the neighborhood store.

Picture a tree-lined street one summer Sunday afternoon in a midwestern city. The neighborhood consists of large, well-kept square houses, characteristic of those popular in the 1920's. Some residents are sitting on their porches, a few are working on the lawn or flower beds. A group of young children are playing on the sidewalk. All are Negro with the exception of one elderly lady who sits on her front porch staring straight ahead. In a matter of months she has become a stranger in the community that had been her home for more than three decades.

The church needs to be aware of the sacrifices it is asking when it requests that laymen remain in a racially changing community indefinitely. It is asking sacrifices which it does not necessarily require of its clergy. The tendency is for the denomination to send pastors with no children to churches located in racially changing neighborhoods. A disproportionate number of pastors serving the churches in this study were bachelors. A large number of the married pastors were young and had no children or else very young children. Another group had grown children who were no longer living at home. Only a few men had school-age children. One minister serving a church in a neighborhood which was rapidly changing commented, "I suppose the main reason we were sent here is because we have no children."

Furthermore, the ministry is an itinerant profession. The clergyman knows that he will in due time move to some other community. He does not have an investment in a house. He may therefore be able to view the situation with more detachment than his laymen.

The laymen feel that although the minister lives in the community he does not have the same stake in the neighborhood that they do. In one racially changing community the pastor and lay leader made a survey to determine the opinions of the members concerning what their church should do about ministering to the Negro residents. Considerable tension existed in the area at the time the survey was made. The results included some rather violently written outbursts by a number of the church members. Considerable criticism was directed against the pastor for his attempt to persuade the congregation to welcome Negroes into the church.

47

One layman returned the questionnaire with a clipping from a local paper describing the crime rate in a section of the city which had already changed from white to Negro:

The Methodist ministers do not own property in the areas they serve. The church members are as a rule homeowners with children who have sacrificed to have a white neighborhood and a church with white people. Please do not destroy all that these working people have built and maintained.

The racially changing community is one in which everybody loses. The departing white residents may lose financially. They will certainly experience the inconvenience connected with moving, and the possibility of relocating in an area which may be farther from their places of employment. Meaningful friendship ties in community groups such as churches may be broken when the residents move to other parts of the city. This may be one of the most significant losses.

The new Negro residents also lose. The same reasons that make the neighborhood attractive for white residents also make it desirable for Negroes, yet many of the favorable community characteristics are lost in the process of transition. The quality of the public school may decline because of the overcrowding resulting from the increased number of children in the new population group. Property may tend to deteriorate. Many new residents have had to assume large mortgages to purchase their houses and have less money to put into maintenance than the former owners, many of whom had their homes completely paid for. The tension which may exist during a period of transition does not add to the safety of the neighborhood. In several communities in which churches in this study are located there have been incidents of violence ranging from broken windows to bombings.

The witness of the Christian church in a racially changing neighborhood is made by the persons who are there at the time. In a real sense they are the church in that community. With all its denominational assemblies, conferences, officials, and pronouncements, the course of the church in the local community is dependent upon the actions of its laymen.

In one instance the witness of the church in the community depended on a middle-aged bricklayer, a retired steelworker, and a housewife. The entire denominational effort in the field of race relations came to focus in that community in the decision that these three persons made. These individuals may have seemed unlikely persons to have had to deal with one of the most difficult issues of the day. With the motivation provided by the Christian faith ordinary people have accomplished extraordinary results. This continues to be true in racially changing communities.

49

It is people like these—the merchants, the housewives, the homeowners, the parents—who in the tense and difficult racially changing neighborhood determine what the witness of the gospel shall be in that situation.

III

RESPONSIBILITY RELINQUISHED

By standards normally used Grace Church should be considered fortunate. The new building is attractive and functional. Furthermore it is debt free. The new parsonage has a mortgage of less than a thousand dollars, and this will be paid within the year.

However, Grace Church has a membership which commutes from many sections of the city. From the predominately Negro neighborhood in which the church is located only one Negro lady attends the

services, and she has not asked—nor has been asked
—to join.

The loyal members make the trip back to Grace
at some personal sacrifice. A bus is provided by the
church for the elderly persons who cannot make
the trip by public transportation or private car.
Recruitment of new members is difficult, as the
nearby Negro residents who would find the church
most convenient are not considered prospects.

The pastor feels "twinges of conscience" because
he is not trying to minister to the residents of the
community. He is convinced, however, that an attempt to bring Negroes into the church would
result in an exodus of enough white members to
threaten the very existence of the congregation.
There is reason for his fears, as the church is made
up of remnants of three congregations which moved
out of Negro communities.

The story of Grace Church began almost eight
years ago when Negroes began moving into a community where there was a neighborhood church
of five hundred members. The congregation decided to sell their white frame building to a Negro
Methodist group and to merge with another church
of almost six hundred members approximately a
mile away.

This was to be a temporary measure, as the
combined congregations purchased a lot on which a
new church building was to be constructed. Before

the new building could be erected Negroes had not only moved into the community around the second church, but they were buying homes in the section where the lot was located. Thus, before the congregation could carry out its plans it was faced with the same problem in regard to the proposed location.

The next step was for the combined congregations to merge with a third church of almost seven hundred members. The second building was sold to a Negro Baptist group. The three congregations then had a total membership of just under eighteen hundred. Two years later it was almost nine hundred and today it is slightly over seven hundred. The strategy was to relocate still farther away, taking the membership and financial assets of the three merged churches. Thus only two years after the first two congregations had merged the third building was sold to a Pentecostal congregation and Grace Church moved less than a mile away and erected the present building.

In the course of less than three years there had been two mergers and the sale of three churches and three parsonages. The congregation had accumulated, through contributions to the building fund and the sale of three churches and parsonages, approximately $200,000 and three electric organs.

At the time the congregation occupied the new building a Negro family moved into a house which adjoined the church. The neighborhood gradually became predominately Negro. Today the congregation is confronted with the same dilemma which some of its members have faced three times before— only now there is no place to relocate.

Reasons for Relocation

The first reaction of a congregation which finds itself in a racially changing community is to consider relocation. The reasons for moving are many and attractive. The members themselves are in the process of relocating their residences. It is only natural that they would prefer taking their church with them. As the community changes it tends to lose its familiar character so that individuals have less desire to return to the church. Furthermore, the old church is in-conveniently located for the people who have moved out and now have to make the time-consuming trip back through city traffic to attend services.

The church leaders may reason that if the church remains at its present location it will die. They are absolutely correct in this conclusion. Unless the church wins adherents from its community, its life is limited to that of the present members who make the effort to return to keep the institution alive. A white congregation in a Negro neighborhood simply cannot recruit a sufficient number of white members to keep the church going indefinitely.

The members are not sure that the Negroes who are moving into the neighborhood want to come to their church. It is rather easy for them to convince themselves that their kind of church program is so different from that of Negro churches that the new-comers could not possibly appreciate it or find it meaningful. That this may not be true is of no conse-quence—the important factor is that the church members feel it is true and act accordingly.

The congregation may also feel that Negroes want to have their own churches. That they have no specific reason for believing this about the persons moving into their community does not prevent the acceptance of this idea.

An item raised by those who are concerned with the financial aspects of the church is the belief that the Negroes could not support their church in the style to which it had been accustomed. It is pointed out that the high cost of maintaining a building as large as theirs would be extremely difficult if the admission of Negroes resulted in the departure of any number of the present substantial contributors. De-spite the fact that the leaders manage to convince themselves that the Negroes who might join "their" church could not manage to support it, they do not hesitate in selling the building to a Negro congrega-tion when the decision to relocate has been made.

Once the congregation is convinced that the church cannot survive at its present location, the decision to seek a new location follows easily. The rapidly ex-panding suburbs in cities with an increasing Negro population provide areas where new congregations are needed. The need for new suburban churches is real. The congregation can easily emphasize the service it is performing by starting a new church and conveniently overlook any responsibility to the community it is leaving.

The fact that a number of the members happen to reside now in the new community which needs a church can speed the decision. Of course, not all members are happy about it. Some find the new location less convenient. A few members still live in the old neighborhood and do not want to see their church leave them behind.

The factor which may finally convince the congregation to relocate is the opportunity to sell its building to a Negro congregation which wishes to move out of a neighborhood close to the center of the city. There are appraisals and negotiations, offers and counteroffers, before a price is agreed upon. The white congregation feels that it is making a real concession in the price, as the amount received is much less than that necessary today to construct a building of comparable size.

A ready market for the church building is probably the most important factor in enabling white congregations to relocate away from racially changing neighborhoods. If a Negro congregation were not eager to purchase the old property, the white members might not have the money to purchase land and erect a new building without actually contributing all the necessary funds themselves. Certainly relocation would be much more difficult if it were not so easy to sell the old property.

Difficulty of Decision

The decision to sell the building and relocate is sometimes made with great reluctance. Many people dislike to see a church which was associated with important events in their lives go out of existence. For many members the sale is like the passing of an old and dear friend. One can understand the ambivalent feelings of a man who votes for relocation and sale of a church in which a stained-glass window was dedicated to the memory of his parents.

But for many the decision to relocate brings a sigh of relief. The burden of carrying on a program with a continually declining membership, the difficulty of meeting the budget, and the strain of commuting back to the church several times a week cause some members to welcome the decision.

The attitude of the denominational administrators toward a relocation varies. In some Methodist annual conferences the policy is to attempt to keep churches in racially changing communities. These conferences consider the local church in relation to the total denominational strategy for the neighborhood. The appointment of a white or Negro pastor depends on the role which the church attempts to carry out in the community. Such a policy may require considerable involvement on the part of the denominational leaders. It includes supervision and guidance and possibly financial subsidy during the period of transition. The decision to keep a church in a racially changing community may commit the denomination to an extensive missionary undertaking.

Some of the relocated congregations in this study moved not only with the support of their denominational administrators but at their suggestion. In one instance where there was a clear need for a new congregation in the city, the pastor of a church in a neighborhood rapidly becoming Negro was called in by his supervisor and urged to see if he could persuade his people to consider relocating. The executive suggested that they merge with a church some distance away in a community that would eventually change racially. The combined congregations would then be able to erect a new building in the section where a new church was needed. The pastor at the time did not feel that the laymen would consider relocating. But he approached the leaders informally and found them receptive to the idea. In due course both buildings were sold and the first unit of the new church constructed.

The relocation of a congregation away from a racially changing area may solve a number of administrative problems. It can provide some financial assets and a nucleus of members to start a new congregation in a section where one is needed. It may solve the problem of finding a minister for a transitional church. It can relieve the pressure on mission funds which may be necessary to keep the church operating in a racially changing community. In short, relocation can provide a way to avoid a difficult ministry.

Possible Purchasers

For the congregation which has decided to move, the major problems is to find a group to purchase the building. For Methodist churches the preference has been to sell it to a Central Jurisdiction (Negro) congregation. The jurisdictional system has provided a framework which has made it easy for a white Methodist congregation to sell its building to a Negro Methodist congregation. The local white group and the denominational leadership then have the satisfaction of knowing that the church is still within the denominational family. This helps relieve possible guilt feelings that any of the white members might have about a responsibility for ministering to the newcomers.

In all fairness it should be pointed out that in many places Negro and white denominational leaders have worked together closely in arranging for the sale of property in light of the overall church strategy. White congregations have sold their buildings to Negro Methodist churches for considerably less than they could have received from other denominational groups. In one instance the white and Negro annual conferences located in the same geographical area worked out a formal procedure for handling property in a changing community.

Despite the examples of cooperation cited above there are cases of white Methodist congregations selling buildings to Negro Methodist congregations for the market value of the property in question. In one instance evidence shows that a Negro Methodist congregation was expected to top the highest bid which a Baptist group had made. Another Negro congregation, after purchasing a building from a white group, discovered its "new" church to be in the path of the expressway extension. The Negro pastor is convinced that the expressway route was known to some of the leaders in the white congregation prior to the sale. The construction of the expressway was a year or two away at the time, and the white congregation was anxious to move.

If there is no possibility of selling the property to another Methodist group, the church is generally sold to the highest bidder. In this study all churches sold were purchased by other church groups. With the exception of the one that subsequently had to be torn down to make room for the freeway, all of the former white Methodist buildings are being used by Negro churches, either Methodist or of some other denomination. While occasionally a church site is valuable as commercial property and can be used as a parking lot or filling station, none of the neighborhood churches in this study fell into that category.

Underlying Issues

The major factor for members of the local church and denominational executives to consider before a church sells its building and relocates is the need for a continuing ministry in the community. In discussing one racially changing community a church leader commented, "This neighborhood has no future." The statement was not correct. What this person really meant was that the community did not have a future as far as white inhabitants were concerned. Every neighborhood left by the relocated congregations in this study has some type of future. The persons involved in the community's future may not be white. The denomination needs to face squarely and honestly the question: What is our responsibility to the people who will be living in the community in the years ahead?

This question must be answered in each local situation. Factors will vary from place to place. The decision should be made in terms of what the future of the community will be after the racial change is complete and what role a church of the particular denomination considering relocating can play in ministering to the inhabitants.

A matter which needs to be pondered in considering relocation is the question of who really owns the church property. The trust clause required in regard to Methodist church property (*Discipline* of The Methodist Church, 1964, paragraph 174) is a useful

61

device for turning the property of a defunct church over to the denomination. However, the issue in a racially changing community involves not a property without a congregation, but in most cases a group of active members.

The membership of a local church, through its Board of Trustees, is responsible for the care of the property. But should the group of people who are members at a particular time have the option of selling the property and moving the assets elsewhere? Legally they can do so subject to certain procedures, such as the approval of the district superintendent and the appraisal of the site by the District Board of Church Location.

The matter becomes more involved when the question is put this way: Does any congregation have the right to leave a residential neighborhood where there are persons living for an indefinite future? In many cases the church building was erected and paid for by a previous generation. The present members have inherited the church property. Is the church building primarily for the use of the persons who happen to be members at this particular time? Is it, or should it be, used for ministering to the residents of the community in which the founders built it?

The relocating congregation needs to realize that it may be primarily moving assets and not members. The new church will generally keep those members who find the new location convenient. Persons who do not live near the new site will tend to transfer to churches in the community where they now live. The loyalty which many members have to the old church will not be transferred to the new church.

The merger of the white and Negro annual conferences in the North and West means that a Methodist congregation wishing to leave a racially changing community can no longer easily sell its building to a Negro Methodist group. It is unlikely that the annual conference administrators will look favorably on the sale of property by one church group to another church group within the same conference. This will tend to prevent the easy retreat of white congregations, and in the long run result in more white churches receiving Negro members.

The merger of the jurisdictions has resulted in some annual conferences getting back churches which were sold to Negro congregations in the Central Jurisdiction. In at least one instance a church sold to a Negro Methodist group returned to the previously all-white annual conference—only now the church has a large mortgage in default. The annual conference is having to assume the payments. One leader commented, "If we hadn't sold the church in the first place we wouldn't have to help pay the mortgage now."

Implications of Sale and Relocation

About ten years ago a white northern church sold its building to a Negro Methodist group, held a mortgage of over $60,000 for the sale, and merged with another white congregation.

Before three years had passed, the Negro community had expanded into the sector where the white church was now located. Instead of selling and moving again it was led by the annual conference to make an effort to win the new residents. Negroes soon began joining the church so that in a few years the community and congregation became predominately Negro. The merger of the jurisdictions in that section of the country placed both this congregation and the Negro Methodist group on the original location in the same annual conference.

The relocated congregation decided to replace its sanctuary and enter into a building campaign. The old sanctuary unit was torn down and a new one erected. This building is partially being paid for by the mortgage payments made by the church on the original location. Thus the second group had their facilities updated partially at the expense of the other one. Practically none of the persons benefiting from the new building are part of the original congregation which sold its building a decade ago.

There seems to be a kind of basic injustice in the situation described above. One church group is clearly reaping where it did not sow. When a church sells and relocates, it is updating its facilities at the expense of the purchaser. The white congregation which sells its old building to a Negro group is trading in its old plant for a new one. The Negro congregation pays for the old church, while the white group gets the new one. It would be interesting to know how many new suburban churches were partially paid for by Negroes who have received an old and perhaps outdated building in return.

An important implication in the sale of a church building is the usefulness of its facilities. Many congregations are aware of the impending racial change and therefore postpone major building repairs. Thus, the Negro group which buys a church may acquire not only a substantial debt, but also get an old building with an accumulation of deferred maintenance. In contrast, the white congregation erects a new building which will need a minimum of maintenance.

Furthermore, the old building may not provide the kind of space suitable for the needed program. In one city a large building, whose memorial windows in German indicated its Lutheran origin, was purchased by a small Negro Methodist congregation. The large meeting rooms proved to be particularly difficult to adapt to the needs of a church school with a large number of young children.

In discussing the sale of church buildings one frequently hears the comment that the selling price was only a fraction of what it would cost to construct a building of comparable size. This is of course true, but it is irrelevant to the issue of building use. The purchasing group, especially if it is a new and struggling congregation, may get a building that is large

THE CHURCH IN THE RACIALLY CHANGING COMMUNITY

and costly to maintain. A new suburban congregation can build one unit at a time, as needed, for a growing membership. The Negro congregation must buy the entire building all at once, whether they need it and can use it or not. The purchase price may be low in terms of replacement costs, but high for what may be an inadequate building for today's needs.

The congregation which relocates has, by moving, written off the neighborhood. In retrospect, was this a valid decision? As has been pointed out, all of the former Methodist buildings are being used by some church group. In a number of instances there is evidence that these congregations are prospering. One building, sold six years ago to a Baptist group, is being extensively remodeled. Another, sold seven years ago to a Pentecostal group, is well maintained and has recently had a new roof installed. In such instances there is every indication that Methodist congregations could have succeeded in these neighborhoods.

In other cases the buildings have deteriorated. A sign which reads, "Church of God in Christ," obviously painted by an amateur or broken windows do not indicate a prospering congregation. It would require mission support to keep a Methodist congregation in certain neighborhoods.

As its community faces the change from white to Negro residents the congregation will inevitably consider the question of whether it should stay or relocate. The issue should not be decided by the ease with which the building can be sold or the need for a down payment on a new suburban church. The basic question to be faced honestly is: When this neighborhood has completed its change, should there be a Methodist church at this location?

IV

FALTERING FORTRESS

"Last year we raised almost $110,000. We have over a thousand members. I don't see what the kingdom of God will gain if we take in Negroes and lose this church." These words were spoken by the pastor of a large congregation with a 100 percent Caucasian membership. The community in which the church is located had become Negro almost nine years ago.

Sometimes a congregation will respond to a racially changing community by acting as though nothing had happened. If such a church survives, it tends to be a large congregation with an impressive building. It may, by virtue of its strength, for a time determine its course and ignore the people in the neighborhood. Such a church becomes a kind of fortress which looks after the persons inside and finds means of protection against those without. But, as with any person or institution that refuses to face reality, there inevitably comes a day when the postponed decision can no longer be avoided. Case histories of two such congregations will be presented.

Temporary Respite

Only a dozen years ago Marcy Avenue Church had the largest membership of any church in the annual conference. From more than 3,300 members the congregation has now declined to slightly over 1,300, but the pastor reports that this figure is approximately 200 higher than the number of names actually on the church records. Despite the membership decline Marcy Avenue is still a comparatively strong congregation. The Sunday morning worship service usually has between 400 and 500 persons present, while the church school for the past year reported an average attendance of just under 500 people.

The community in which the church is located was developed during the 1920's, as evidenced by the large number of square two-story houses popular during that period. Negroes began moving into the

69

area in the mid-1950's. By the time the present pastor came to the church eight years ago the neighborhood was almost completely inhabited by Negroes. The nearby high school had a more than 95 percent Negro enrollment.

Over the years the church has considered the white membership its major responsibility. From time to time Negro visitors have attended the Sunday morning services. The pastor reports that between seventy-five and one hundred Negroes have attended services in the eight years that he has served the church. He reported more Negro visitors during the first four years of his ministry there than during the last four years. Negro guests are sent cards of welcome, but the minister of membership does not call on Negro visitors as he does on the white visitors. There are no Negroes attending church school.

An important factor to be considered in the future course of Marcy Avenue is the continued change in the neighborhood. When the community first changed from white to Negro, the new residents were largely middle-class persons who were very much like the people moving away. As the number of Negroes in the city increased, however, and as urban renewal forced the movement of many persons living in older sections close to the downtown, the community around Marcy Avenue Church has changed again. The economically successful persons who first moved into the area have tended to move farther on. Lower status Negroes have been moving in, with the result that the community in general shows signs of over-crowding and deterioration.

The community has gone through two kinds of changes. It first changed from a middle-class white to a middle-class Negro, then to a lower-class Negro area. The large, imposing Marcy Avenue Church, which once catered to middle-class whites, may find it very difficult, if not impossible, to serve the residents of this community.

The deterioration of the community has resulted in some disorder. The pastor reports that there have been three purse snatchings and one holdup on the corner where the church is located. The congregation hires off-duty uniformed police officers for $2 per hour to provide protection for evening meetings. There is a regular schedule of evening meetings where such protection is provided. Eight adult church school classes have meetings once a month, but these groups must arrange for the officer to be on duty if they so desire. Four police officers who are members of the church are hired when they are needed and available.

The church staff and lay members have made a real effort to cultivate the white members and to win others. There is in addition to the senior pastor a retired minister who does calling and supervises the zone plan whereby members living in the various communities around the city are organized into groups. A seminary student is employed part time to work with the youth. Two secretaries comprise the office staff.

There are several large churches of other denominations in the Marcy Avenue community. The Baptist congregation, the only church of that denomination in the city, has been able to keep many of its members, although even here the total has dropped from about 3,000 to 2,000. Currently it has only one Negro member, a seventeen-year-old high school girl. A Presbyterian church with a membership of just under 1,000 has an integrated church school. The present pastor, who has been on the scene for a little under a year, came with the avowed purpose of integrating the church but has not met with any unusual success. This church operates a day nursery which serves only Negro children, but none of the parents have been persuaded to join the church.

The leadership of Marcy Avenue Church is thinking of the future, but not in terms of the future of the immediate neighborhood. The pastor reports: "A few years ago we realized that the church couldn't go on here indefinitely. We decided that we should start raising funds to be used in accordance with the best judgment at such a time as a decision has to be made." The congregation has been putting aside a sum of money each year. Currently a little over $100,000 is in this account. In addition the congregation anticipates receiving more than $70,000 in bequests. The pastor describes his hopes for the future as follows:

Sooner or later this property will be disposed of, and the funds the church will have then can be used to start new congregations—at least two, but I hope three. We have about ten years yet—five years of reasonably satisfactory service, then five years of struggle. At that time we will have to do something. Integration is a possibility, but this state is far more southern than northern.

Missed Opportunity

"The church can't be maintained indefinitely. I give it about two years." This was the new minister's diagnosis of Johnson Park Church at the end of his first three months.

Johnson Park Church has slightly over four hundred members. Its well-maintained stone sanctuary is fifty years old, while the large educational building was erected twenty-five years ago. The neighborhood never had more inhabitants than today, yet the pastor gives the church only two years to live.

Johnson Park Church has continued to minister to white people only, despite the fact that Negroes began moving into the community almost fifteen years ago. The Negro residents in the community have been in the majority for almost a decade.

Prior to the movement of Negroes into the Johnson Park community the church had over twelve hundred members, three times the present membership. The minister who came to the church at the time of the racial change stayed for more than a decade. He reported, "We never considered selling the church. We managed to hold our members until their children reached junior high school—then they transferred." The decline in membership has been slow but steady. Many of the remaining four hundred members are persons over sixty years of age. Less than one hundred still live in the Johnson Park community.

The congregation never adopted a formal policy regarding a ministry to Negroes. The man who served as pastor during and after the community change reported that while the subject was certainly discussed informally, it was never brought up for consideration by the official board. Occasionally a Negro has attended the Sunday service; none has ever returned.

Four other Protestant churches in the community have been sold to Negro congregations. The nearby Roman Catholic Church and parochial school serve a predominately Negro constituency. Only Johnson Park Church has retained a 100 percent white membership.

The age of the members and the distance between their residences and the church has resulted in very few church activities. The church school has only two classes, one for men and one for women. There have been no children in the church school for several years. The former pastor's wife is a director of Christian education. When there were no longer any children in the church school, she utilized her training by accepting a position in another church across town. The educational building has more than a dozen classrooms with some of the best-waxed floors in the denomination.

The regularly scheduled activities include the Woman's Society with its various circles, and the official board which meets monthly. The Sunday morning service and the church school with two classes are the only regular weekly activities.

The church staff consists of the senior pastor, a student assistant pastor, a church secretary, and a full-time sexton. The budget for the current year is slightly over $30,000. Consideration is being given to having the pastor spend a portion of his time organizing a church in the suburbs. The Johnson Park building may ultimately be sold and the assets transferred to the proposed new church. The plans are not clear at this time.

The future of Johnson Park Church is not encouraging. It could not now integrate easily even if it should decide to do so. The neighborhood has changed long ago, and the residents by now have established church relationships. To try to establish a Negro congregation now would be as difficult as to start a new church in a suburb ten years after the community had developed.

Furthermore there is considerable question as to whether the congregation could find a buyer for the building should it desire to sell. From the selfish point of view of getting the maximum price for the building, the time to have sold was when the area was changing. With four other Negro Protestant congregations nearby it is doubtful whether another Negro group might wish to face the competition in attempting to locate in the community.

Johnson Park Church has ignored the community around it for over a decade. The church has long passed the point when it could have decided to continue serving in its present location or to relocate. The day of reckoning is almost at hand.

The Fortress Church

The church which attempts to serve only white persons, even though the neighborhood around it becomes Negro, is one which in effect shuts out the community for which it has primary responsibility. It may shut out the newcomers by deliberately excluding them or by not bothering to seek them out and invite them to attend. The church adapts its program to a white constituency residing largely outside of the community.

A church which survives as a white congregation for any length of time after its community has become predominately Negro must have a large membership at the time the neighborhood changes so that the church can lose a substantial number and still survive. Thus a church of 2,500 members may lose half of the persons on the roll and still remain a thriving institution. It may have to reduce program and staff, but with over a thousand members it is hardly in danger of closing.

Often a large congregation in a racially changing

community still thinks of itself as the great church it used to be. The members have difficulty realizing that their church is declining. The tradition of strength tends to persist even after the strength no longer exists. One such congregation, now barely one third the size it was fifteen years ago, is considering extensive remodeling. The chairman of the board, an energetic gentleman in his mid-seventies, is heartily in favor of the remodeling. He talks enthusiastically about the "spirit of Asbury church." Yet the church is now in a Negro neighborhood, serving an all-white commuting membership.

One of the reasons why large congregations are able to survive for a time in Negro neighborhoods is that they have always had a number of members coming from a distance. Some people have considered the varied program well worth the trouble of traveling some distance to the church. Consequently the congregation always was less dependent on its immediate neighborhood than a smaller church would be. The momentum thus gathered propels the church forward for a period of time.

For two practical reasons a large congregation may find difficulty in relocating out of a racially changing neighborhood. First, there may be no place to go which will be satisfactory to a large number of people. The small congregation of two hundred or three hundred members may find a site convenient to half of them. Such a church can relocate, leaving the remaining members to find places in other churches more

77

conveniently situated. However, the problem is magnified when fifteen hundred members are involved. So large a church may be willing to relocate, feeling that it can recruit replacements from the new community. But if it may lose five hundred or more members by relocating it will ponder the matter seriously before making the move.

Second, there may be no market for the old building. Many large congregations have enormous facilities for which they can find no buyer. The small neighborhood church can usually, if it does not wait too long, find a Negro congregation which wants to purchase its building. Because the facilities are modest the Negro group can raise enough money for a down payment and secure a loan for the balance of the purchase price. If the church plant is so large that a half million dollars would be considered a low figure, the problem of finding a purchaser can be extremely difficult. Only a Negro congregation of some strength could consider such a purchase. Furthermore the Negro congregation which is large and wealthy enough to purchase a half-million-dollar building could erect a new building of its own.

Some white congregations in neighborhoods now populated by Negroes are there only because they cannot find Negro groups to whom they could sell their large church buildings. In one instance a large building with only a small white congregation remaining was to be sold to a Negro church of another denomination. The Negro group had a building near the center of the city which it anticipated selling as a site for an office building. All arrangements were made, and a price of slightly under a half million dollars was agreed upon. The white congregation had arranged to merge with a suburban church. The assets from the sale were to provide the suburban church with a badly needed sanctuary unit. A few days before the contract was signed the business group which had planned to purchase the Negro church for an office building decided against it. As a result the small white congregation, six years later, still meets in the same large building.

The church which attempts to serve only a white constituency although located in a Negro neighborhood must make a number of adjustments in its program. Some activities are discontinued, such as Scout programs which tend to be centered in the neighborhood. Weekday activities will be at a minimum. The children's choir may arrange to have its practice on Sunday morning.

A church of this type may place great emphasis on a strong pulpit. Much attention will be given to the musical program. The quality of the Sunday service is considered one of the major factors in persuading the members to come to church.

The focus of the program will be the continued cultivation of the present membership. Individuals may get a great deal of attention from their pastor. With a minimum number of prospective members to contact, the minister turns his time and energy to the persons already on the church roll. Because of their relationship to the pastor the members are less likely to transfer. They may take advantage of a change of pastors to transfer to a more convenient church. Since they do not want to hurt the pastor's feelings they leave simultaneously with him, and before they can get to know the new man. A pastor appointed to such a church reported that the week he arrived nineteen families, representing almost fifty members, transferred.

A large church which continues for a while in a changed neighborhood must have competent leadership in order to survive. It can secure a capable preacher, at least at the beginning. However, the pastor of such a church tends to direct his efforts toward maintaining the institution. In a number of cases the minister was quick to point out the substantial contribution his church was making to missions and other denominational causes, implying that the admission of Negroes would result in an exodus of white members and a loss of support to the denomination.

The membership of the church, at least in the early days of existence as a white congregation in a Negro community, provides an adequate work load for the minister or ministers. The task of calling on members who now live a distance from the church is a time-consuming activity. A pastor reported that in one day he made eight calls on his members. To do so required six hours and seventy-two miles of driving.

The lay leadership of a white church in a Negro neighborhood like to maintain the church as they have known it. During the period of neighborhood change there may be considerable anxiety about the future of the church. During this period many of the members themselves are moving away. However, after the change is complete and the church continues and even appears to prosper despite some loss of members, the situation tends to stabilize. The congregation adjusts to having a commuting constituency. Finally the decline reaches a point where all participants are conscious of the fact that the church cannot survive over a long-term future. This period is characterized by a feeling of apathy. Friendship ties hold the congregation together. It is a particularly difficult time for the pastor. He, even more than the members, sees the church as a holding operation, but he does not have the long-term ties and friendships which for some of the laymen may provide an adequate reason for the church's existence.

The fortress church is an enigma to the denominational administrators. Such a church is less subject to outside pressure than is the smaller neighborhood congregation. It has been and still is a strong church with the sense of independence that strength engenders. It can and does hire a competent preacher. It can pay all its bills and denominational requests. Until such a church declines to the point where it can no longer secure a minister or continue to be self-supporting, the denomination can do little other than urge and exhort. A more detailed account of the results of denominational pressure will be given in chapter VII.

The church which continues as a white island in a Negro community may present a problem in the city for the entire denomination. Such a church becomes a symbol of exclusion for the denomination because it has set a standard. Negroes who would be potential members of churches of the same denomination may judge the entire denomination in light of this large, prominent, and exclusive congregation.

Another embarrassment to the denomination is the tendency of other congregations in racially changing communities to follow example. These churches may see an all-white congregation ignoring its Negro neighborhood and seeming to be successful. It may be looked upon as a model by churches which otherwise might follow a different course. If other congregations follow a similar policy, they too will pass the crucial time for making the decision which will determine if the church loses or saves its life.

Outlook for the Future

A white congregation can survive in a Negro neighborhood only for a while. The length of the time will vary depending on such circumstances as the initial strength of the church, the distance the members must travel, and the ability of the minister. The ultimate end is the same. The church dies.

The collapse may come rather quickly after a time

of seeming stability. One church in the study which had been going along fairly well lost a number of members, and in one year was forced to reduce the pastor's salary by $1,800. This resulted in a change of pastors, the securing of a part-time minister, and the hastening of the collapse.

The congregation which postpones its decision will reach a time when it no longer can make a choice about its future. There may be no market for the building, so the church cannot relocate. The time may have passed when such a church could successfully win Negro members. Most residents will already have found a convenient church. Furthermore Negroes are not likely to come to a church which has excluded them for several years. The neighborhood may have continued to change from one Negro social class group to another, so that there is an almost unbridgeable gap between the white congregation and the persons living in the community.

The congregation which ignores its community cannot survive over a long term. The eventual result is the death of the church, not through an assault from without but by a lack of new life within.

V

DIE TO LIVE

The first thing I did was to let them know that I had been sent there to serve all people. I said, "If you're a closed corporation, let me know and I won't do anything for this year and will ask to be transferred next year." If the chairman of the board hadn't stayed, I doubt if we would have made it. The lay leader was reluctant, but he said, "We've got to do this even if we don't like it."

It [integration] grew a lot like Topsy. We didn't proselyte at the beginning as the large Negro churches claimed. We just welcomed them. A Negro woman who had been singing in the choir wanted to join. One day the pastor called and said, "Shall we take it to the official board?" I said, "Yes, if you want a row. We've no right to deny them membership." The pastor said, "That's just what I thought you'd say."

I know many Negroes who fear and distrust whites. They feel that the whites are not showing their true side when they invite Negroes to come to their church.

The above comments are from a pastor, a white layman, and a Negro layman in the same church—a church in which the membership is now approximately 50 percent Negro. They illustrate some of the hopes and ambitions, the fears and insecurities of those who attempt to guide a congregation through a period of racial change.

The congregation which decides to stay and attempt to minister to all the residents in a racially changing community embarks on an uncharted course. Neither pastor nor layman may have a clear idea of what their church expects as it attempts to seek Negro members. Case histories of three congregations which have survived and serve in racially changing neighborhoods will be presented in this chapter.

Inclusive by Choice

A congregation was singing the familiar words, "In suffering Thou hast made us one."

The 120 persons in attendance at Memorial Church

that Sunday morning might have been typical of any city congregation. However, about half of the worshipers were Negro. Memorial has been an inclusive congregation for several years. The proportion of Negro members has been increasing. Two years ago approximately 40 percent of the members were Negroes. Today the congregation is evenly divided between Negroes and Caucasians.

Race is not the only difference between the membership groups. The casual observer will note that there are very few white members who appear to be under sixty years of age. There are no white teen-agers and only three young adults. In contrast, with the exception of one elderly couple, all Negro worshipers appear to be under forty years old.

Memorial Church is in its period of maximum inclusiveness, at least in regard to the proportion of Negro and white members. It has taken almost a decade for the congregation to reach this point. The church illustrates the unique opportunities and problems inherent in interracial membership.

Memorial Church is located in a well-maintained residential neighborhood. The church building, a white frame structure, was erected almost sixty years ago when the congregation moved to the present site. The facilities include a sanctuary, an educational wing, and a gymnasium. The building has been kept in excellent repair.

Negroes began moving into the neighborhood almost ten years ago. The change in the community has been gradual and orderly. There was no period of panic or block-busting. However, the proportion of the Negro residents has increased considerably in the past couple of years. Two years ago the enrollment of a large elementary school two blocks from the church was only 30 percent Negro. Today over 90 percent of the pupils are Negro. The pastor and his family are the only white residents in their block.

The neighborhood was predominately white when the Negroes began attending Memorial Church. The first family consisted of a lady and her three young daughters. The girls began coming to the church school. Later their mother started coming to worship. The pastor commented, "The little girls were very cute; this helped. The family was accepted, although not by everyone." Some persons went out of their way to be cordial while others were unfriendly. One Sunday a white family moved to another place in the sanctuary when the Negro family sat down with them.

A few Negroes joined over a three-year period, but the number of Negro children attending the church school increased until they constituted a majority. A change of pastors brought a man who was committed to ministering to Negroes. He was successful in recruiting a number into the church. He persuaded teams of one Negro and one white member to do visitation evangelism bringing more Negroes into the congregation.

The increase in the number of Negro partici-pants was not without effect on the white constituency. By the time a number of Negroes began attending, the majority of white members had moved out of the neighborhood. Others took this occasion to transfer their membership.

The first group of whites to leave were families with teen-age children. An instance of interracial dating had occurred which resulted in the immediate withdrawal of white families with children in the Junior and Senior Youth Fellowships. One white layman commented, "The white people with teen-age children have moved away and taken their membership for fear of interracial marriage."

Despite the loss of members the church has prospered financially. It still has the support of a number of loyal members who travel back to their old neighborhood. Furthermore the Negro members have been contributing substantially. The church has always had a reputation for strong fellowship. The pastor commented, "The Negro members have adopted this loyalty, even financially." Six Negro families tithe, contributing between $600 and $700 each. Of the five largest contributors three are Negroes. The current budget is over $20,000. Subsidy from the denomination has not been necessary.

As more Negroes joined the church the number elected to positions of leadership on various commissions and committees increased. One of the last groups to which Negroes were elected was the finance commission. It, too, now has an inclusive membership.

The members of the congregation have come to

know one another as individuals by holding various commission meetings in one another's homes. One Negro member commented on the strong fellowship which has developed within the Memorial congregation and felt that the meetings held in homes had contributed to it. He said, "You don't really get to know people at church but only as you get into one another's homes. If a person thinks enough of you to invite you into his home he really thinks something of you."

The white members of the congregation now know and like the Negro members as individuals. There are laymen in the church who are warm and cordial to the Negro members whom they know, but of whom the pastor says, "The mention of the NAACP and CORE makes them apoplectic."

An interesting incident illustrates how the feeling of the white members toward Negroes in general may contrast with their attitude toward the Negroes in the church membership whom they know as individuals. Approximately a year ago a boycott of the public schools to protest de facto segregation was attempted. The group sponsoring it wanted to use the church as a "freedom station." The Negro children who were boycotting the school were to come to the church and listen to lectures on civil rights and Negro history. The white pastor was to be in charge of the program at the church.

The issue of whether or not the church was to be used as the "freedom station" was brought before the official board. Some of the Negroes on the board were not in sympathy with the school boycott but did not want to oppose it by refusing the use of their church. None of the white board members were in sympathy with the boycott. After considerable discussion the issue came to a vote. The white board members abstained from voting rather than hurt the feelings of the Negro members.

During the period when Negroes were beginning to join the church, several key laymen supported the pastor in his effort to win Negro members. An important part was played by a retired banker who had been a member of the church for over half a century. When the church leaders were struggling with the question of whether to welcome Negroes into their fellowship, this layman took a strong, positive position in support of the pastor and exerted an important influence on other white members. In commenting on his experiences in the interracial congregation he said, "This is the greatest opportunity we have had in the fifty years I have been a member. I have never felt that a work was more worth supporting than I have here."

The pastor feels that the congregation is looked upon by the residents of the neighborhood in general as a "white church that integrated" rather than a Negro congregation. He also reports that there has been some pressure on his Negro members by their neighbors trying to discourage them from attending Memorial Church. He says that the phrase "white lover" has been used by some Negro residents to refer in a derogatory way to his Negro members.

So far the congregation has achieved a successfully inclusive fellowship. In speaking of the future the pastor said, "Up until two years ago most people felt that the church would die. Now even if the white congregation should leave, the church won't die off as it would have just a few years ago."

The Cycle Completed

A Boy Scout troop was being organized in Wesley Church. As part of the publicity the pastor sent a letter to the schools in the area announcing the formation of the troop and inviting all interested boys to attend a meeting at the church.

The meeting brought a shock to the church. Several Negro boys who received the invitation in school were interested in scouting and came. No Negroes were then living in the immediate vicinity of the church, and a neighborhood "Improvement Association" was working to see that the community remained white.

The presence of the Negro boys brought the church to the realization of what was to take place in their community. The Negro community at that time was still some distance away. The "Improvement Association" was watching its southward movement with apprehension, but the church people just had not faced the possibility of racial change. With the Negro children sitting in the fellowship hall the trend was clear. The congregation was forced to consider their responsibility in a changing community before the change actually took place. There was time to discuss, to think through the issues, and to plan for an uncertain future.

The attendance of the Negro boys resulted in the appointment of a nine-member Social Concerns Commission representing various viewpoints. The group issued the following policy statement: "We recommend that we do not go out seeking people of other races to come into the church, but no one shall be turned away from the church for any reason."

Within a few months after the adoption of this policy a new pastor came to Wesley Church. The first matter with which he had to deal was the possible relocation of the parsonage. The minister's home was some distance from the church in a neighborhood which by then was almost all Negro. Some of the members wanted to relocate the parsonage completely outside the area in a section which would be all white for an indefinite future. The pastor did not really want to move the parsonage at all, but consented to the purchase of a house within a block of the church. He wanted to be identified with the community and felt that living there would help accomplish this goal.

During the next two years an attempt was made to convince the members that the church should seek to minister to all persons in the neighborhood. After a year the policy of not inviting Negroes to the church was formally rescinded. A calling program was started before Negroes moved into the area around the church. Some members, realizing that Negroes would soon be moving into the area, questioned the wisdom of their campaign. It was, however, pointed out that door-to-door evangelism has always been a valid way of reaching persons outside the church, and that such a campaign would indicate, to the benefit of community morale, that the church was not planning to move. In retrospect this campaign had an additional value: No one could later say, "Why should we call on the Negro people? We have never made such calls before."

Two years after the Negro boys attended the Boy Scout meeting the neighborhood around the church began changing. With financial support from the denomination a Negro assistant pastor, a seminary student, was hired on a part-time basis. The reception of the first Negro members coincided with the hiring of this assistant pastor although the two events were not related.

During this period the pastor had been working closely with the church members, attempting to get them to see that the mission of the church is to minister to the residents of its parish. It was not an easy task. The church membership declined as more and more white members moved away. However there were conversions, and individuals caught the challenge of the possibility of their church bridging racial barriers. One elderly member of the board had been born and raised in the Deep South. At first he was very much opposed to the thought of Negroes coming to the church. After a time he said to the pastor, "This is against everything I have been taught. I'm still not sure I agree with what you are trying to do, but I'm not going to oppose it. I'll go along with you." The pastor felt that this statement represented a conversion.

After the Negro assistant pastor had been working for a year, only thirty-seven Negroes had joined the church, making up about 10 percent of the total membership. At this time the attendance at the Sunday morning worship service was made up of 70 percent white and 30 percent Negro persons.

At the beginning of the transition the congregation had over six hundred members. By the time the Negroes began to join, the membership had decreased to approximately three hundred. However, the congregation never dwindled to the point where it was ever in serious financial difficulty. The denomination provided some assistance for emergency building repairs and for the salary of the assistant pastor.

For a time the congregation consisted of both Negro and white members. During this period the members had a sense of mission and fellowship. The pastor commented on the first inclusive picnic held in one of the public parks on the outskirts of the city as an example of the fellowship. The picnic was a complete success, but it caused "some raised eyebrows on the part of other picnickers."

Gradually the neighborhood in which the church is

located attracted more and more Negro residents. The white members of the congregation commuted to church and eventually dwindled away. Now, seven years after the prospective Boy Scouts attended the meeting, the church has 295 members, only seven of whom are white. A Negro senior pastor has served the congregation for almost two years.

Some of the Negro members have expressed disappointment that the congregation has not remained inclusive. For the first time the members of the church had really become acquainted with persons of the other race. A fellowship had developed that some participants had not known before. This was lost as the community and the congregation ultimately became all Negro. The congregation now has nothing to distinguish itself from a typical neighborhood church in a large city.

Denominational Intervention

In its day one of the most desirable streets on which to live in the entire city was the Boulevard. Even today it is an attractive wide street with large trees and is lined by mansions of another era. When the community was being developed during the first decade of this century, St. John Church, already a congregation for twenty years, relocated on a prominent corner. The red brick sanctuary was built at that time, while the gymnasium and some additional classrooms were constructed in the mid-1930's. For over half a century it was one of the prominent churches in the city.

Although located in a residential community St. John has not primarily been a neighborhood-centered church in recent years. It was a congregation noted for its theological conservatism and revival tradition. The emphasis on revivalism is indicated by the fact that one of the pastors had some of the front pews removed so as to have more room for persons who responded to altar calls. Because of its particular theological and program emphases, St. John Church attracted persons from many sections of the city.

In the early 1950's Negroes began moving into the community. No effort was made to welcome these newcomers into the church. At one time YMCA groups were denied the use of the church gymnasium because both Negro and white youth were involved. A white neighborhood organization, however, whose avowed purpose was to keep the community white, was permitted to hold meetings in the church building. St. John Church, consequently, was the last congregation in the area to open its doors to Negroes, and that only under pressure from denominational leaders. The Lutheran and Presbyterian churches in the community had Negroes in their membership long before St. John. Eight years ago when it seemed clear to all that the neighborhood would ultimately be entirely Negro, the congregation proposed to sell its building and merge with a suburban congregation.

The sale and merger would have taken place had

it not been for the intervention of the resident bishop who appointed a special committee to study the situation and make recommendations. Members of the committee included representatives from the local church, the City Missionary Society, the conference, the Board of Missions, and the district. After several meetings the committee recommended that the denomination should maintain a church in the community. They also recommended that the City Missionary Society be prepared to provide the necessary subsidy for enabling the church to minister to the residents in its immediate vicinity. The district superintendent indicated that he supported the recommendation of the committee, and that under no circumstances would he sign the necessary papers to allow the church to be sold. The pastor who was strongly in favor of relocating moved shortly thereafter to another congregation.

The next pastor was a man determined to minister to the Negroes living in the area. He is said to have been as effective in "scaring off many of the white members as he was in bringing Negroes into the congregation." In all probability many of the white members, realizing that they were no longer going to maintain the church as a white congregation, transferred their membership to churches in areas where they were now living.

The pastor stayed only three years. An older white pastor and a young Negro assistant pastor were appointed to the church. The senior pastor held a somewhat conservative theological position which has led some people to suspect that the bishop appointed him to provide the liaison between the older conservative members and the Negroes who it was hoped would soon be taken into membership.

At the time that the church received a biracial staff, the congregation was more than 95 percent white. Only four Negro families were in the congregation of more than three hundred members. The presence of a Negro pastor on the staff did not result in the immediate influx of any appreciable number of Negro members. He began his work in June. The following Easter, nine months later, the group attending the Easter service was approximately 90 percent white. For several years the church had been known in the community as a place where Negroes were not particularly welcome. It could not easily change the image it had created.

An incident on a particular Sunday seemed to be the "tipping point" from a white to a Negro congregation. It was during a Sunday service with special recognition of the Girl Scout troops. Between sixty and seventy Girl Scouts with their leaders and parents came to the service. For the first time the Sunday morning congregation had a definite majority of Negroes in attendance. The pastor felt that many of the white members who had never faced up to the reality that the congregation would someday become predominately Negro saw the trend clearly. A large

number of white persons transferred their membership shortly thereafter.

The congregation has had a Negro pastor now for
almost two years. The membership of under three
hundred is 70 percent Negro and 30 percent white.
A number of loyal white members have stayed with
the church and given it the benefit of leadership,
skills, and financial support.

The present pastor, who came as the Negro assistant minister four years ago, told of the ambivalent
feelings of many of the white members during the
period of transition. He indicated that while many
of these persons could intellectually accept the fact
that the neighborhood had become Negro and that
the church would ultimately follow in this course,
they had "real emotional misgivings about the situation. They felt that the Negroes were needed if the
church was to survive, but they also resented the
Negroes coming."

The last organization to accept Negroes was the
Woman's Society of Christian Service. The main
reason was that the circles had members who had
transferred to other churches but were still active in
the Woman's Society at St. John. The circles met
almost clandestinely. Announcement of time and
place of the meetings never appeared in the church
bulletin. It had been the custom of the pastor's wife
to attend the circle meetings. The Negro pastor's
wife, however, was never invited nor even informed

of the time and place. Finally she decided to "crash one of the circle meetings" and was subsequently invited to attend.

The same church used to have a white high school youth group and a Negro junior high school group. When pressure was put on the high school group to receive Negroes into its membership it disbanded. The adult advisor transferred her membership to another church. Most of the white high school youth group members lived in the area near the church although the advisor did not. Since that time the youth program has had only Negro participants.

The church is currently served by a Negro senior pastor and a white assistant student pastor. It is highly subsidized, receiving more than half of its support from denominational mission funds. The present membership of 250 is the lowest figure reported since the neighborhood began changing more than a decade ago.

A sign on the side of the church building shows two clasped hands, one Negro and the other white. The words underneath read, "All welcome." It is the message which St. John Church is now trying to convey to its community. The damage done by several years of exclusiveness has taken its toll. The denomination is paying a high price in missionary subsidy to keep the church operating while it attempts to win the nearby residents who once were willfully excluded.

The Future of Racially Changing Communities

The preceding case histories are illustrations of what happens to a church which elects or is forced to stay in a racially changing neighborhood. There are three general phases.

In the first phase the congregation struggles with its responsibility to the newcomers. This period is crucial because at this time the decision to stay or relocate is made. If the decision is to stay, an effort to win Negro members follows, a few of whom finally join the church. White members who object to being part of an inclusive congregation leave. Families with children, particularly teen-agers, are among the first to go.

In the second phase the number of Negro members increases to the point where the congregation takes on an interracial character. By the time this phase is reached the neighborhood has a high proportion of Negro residents. The pupils in the church school, with the exception of the adult department, are almost all Negro. The congregation is made up of older adults and young Negro families. However, the members have a sense of accomplishment and a feeling of pride in being part of an interracial fellowship. Some white and Negro members, for the first time in their lives, get to know persons of other races as individuals.

The third and final phase of the process is the gradual withdrawal of white members which finally results in a Negro congregation. The white members already live outside the immediate neighborhood. Many are older persons who find it increasingly difficult to commute back to the church. No new white members can be recruited, so the number remaining gets smaller and smaller. The result is an all-Negro congregation in a Negro neighborhood. The members are disappointed in having their church become "just another ordinary congregation."

The local church is more dependent on the fortunes of the community in which it is located than most church leaders would like to admit. By and large most people tend to join churches convenient to their places of residence. The church program expects the individual members of a family to be at the church at different times during the week for committee meetings, choir rehearsals, men's, women's, and children's meetings, and for special services. It is difficult for the average family with school-age children to participate fully and consume much time driving back and forth to the church. For the sake of friendship and loyalty a member who has moved away may make the sacrifice to return. However, when he decides to transfer his membership, he will select a congregation to his liking that is conveniently located to his place of residence.

The pattern of church attendance described above is significant in understanding the church in the racially changing neighborhood. Urban neighborhoods in America tend to be either all white, all Negro, or in the process of changing from white to

Negro. The change may take place in a matter of months or take several years. In most cases the result is a Negro neighborhood. The furor over de facto school segregation has been caused by the attempt to keep the school integrated while the geographically defined district in which the pupils live is inhabited by only one racial group. The school authorities can require pupils to be transported to a school not of their choosing. Church members will attend the church of their choice.

Every inclusive neighborhood church in this study is, like the community in which it is located, a congregation in transition. None of them are recruiting white members to replace those who die or move away. Several pastors are making a heroic effort to keep their congregations inclusive, but even in these instances the long-term trend seems clear. Eventually the membership will be entirely Negro. As long as Negroes and whites live in separate communities an inclusive neighborhood church cannot be maintained indefinitely.

However, the policy of keeping the church in the community is infinitely more desirable than that of selling the property and relocating. It provides for the gradual development of a Negro congregation which can eventually take over the ministry in the neighborhood without assuming a mortgage necessary to purchase a building. More important, it enables persons of different races to get to know each other as individuals. Even if the population movement does not result in the kind of interracial communities which permit the inclusive church to exist for a long period of time, some individuals have had a learning experience which they will never forget. One of the members of Memorial Church described earlier in this chapter returned to her home in Kansas for a visit of several months. When she returned she said, "You know, I never thought I'd say this, but I missed the integrated congregation."

The exception to the pattern described above is the community where the presence of an institution keeps some white people living in the area. In a few instances a university which could not possibly relocate has provided a sort of anchor for the community. A white housing market for faculty, students, and other university employees is guaranteed. Thus the neighborhood stabilizes without becoming entirely Negro. Churches in such communities have managed to serve an inclusive membership for a number of years, and there is every indication that they will continue to do so. These, however, are the exception and not the rule.

VI

THE TIME IS NEVER RIGHT

A pastor was discussing the future of his church which was located in a racially changing community. More than half of the inhabitants of the immediate neighborhood were Negroes although the congregation was entirely white. In discussing what the church might do in this particular situation the minister indicated that in about a year and a half the congregation should begin to receive Negro members. He stated, "Now the time is not right for integrating the church."

In a certain sense the pastor was correct. The time is never "right" for integrating a church, just as there is no "right" time for making a trip to the dentist or for doing something that the individual would much prefer to avoid. Nevertheless, life is filled with events that demand decisions and actions however unpleasant they may seem.

The congregation which finds itself in a racially changing community frequently has no idea what it ought to do. It has had no experience in dealing with this particular situation. No one involved may even have any knowledge of how other congregations in similar circumstances responded. The lack of a clear course to follow may result in the church drifting until it has gone beyond the point where it can control its direction.

The experiences of the congregations in this study show that some churches do manage to survive and serve in a racially changing community. They can be helpful to those which face similar situations. Even churches which have failed provide valuable information in understanding the results of certain courses of action. This chapter will attempt to show factors, including the role of clergy and laymen, which helped churches remain and minister in racially changing communities.

The Pastor

The key figure in the success or failure of a church to minister in a racially changing community is the minister. He, probably more than any other person, guides the congregation in the direction that it will take. His commitment to the ideal of the church remaining in the community and ministering to all its residents is essential. Even if the pastor himself is committed to this goal he may not be able to persuade the laymen to follow his leading. However, if he is not convinced that this is the course for the church to follow, the congregation will not go against his will. In no church did the congregation attempt to win Negro members against the wishes of the pastor.

The minister who successfully develops an inclusive congregation is likely to be very close to his people. He is a "pastor," a shepherd of the flock. He is keenly sensitive to the fears and anxieties of his members. He develops a close relationship with his members so that they sense his genuine concern. One pastor who has successfully developed an inclusive congregation spoke about the need to do a great deal of pastoral calling, particularly during the early stages of the transition. Another minister spoke of the need "to keep close to the people, particularly those who are opposed to what you are trying to do."

The pastors who were serving inclusive congregations were asked about their degree of involvement in the civil rights movement, particularly their participation in such organizations as the NAACP. All of the men indicated that they were in sympathy with the civil rights movement. Some, but not all, held membership in civil rights organizations. However, none held an office in such a group. None were giving any appreciable amount of their time to the work of the civil rights organizations. All of them considered their churches to be their major concern.

An interesting phenomenon was the lack of any outspoken crusader for liberal causes among the group of pastors who have successfully developed inclusive congregations. In fact some of the worst failures occurred in churches where the pastor viewed himself and was looked upon by his colleagues as a liberal crusader. In one instance a pastor who during his entire ministry had been known as an outspoken advocate of civil rights was sent to a church in a racially changing community. The result of his efforts was the alienation of practically everyone, both white and Negro, and a marked decline in the church.

In some instances the crusading pastor appears to have demanded action on the part of his people before they had developed confidence in him. In such cases the people demanded that the minister move. In some churches the pastor became so alienated from the congregation that it would have been useless for him to remain. One pastor was working to bring Negro members into the church against the will of the white congregation. The community was just beginning to change racially, and many residents hoped the Negro influx would not occur. The Pastoral Relations Committee met in the pastor's absence to discuss whether they wanted him to continue beyond his first year. The group decided that they would invite the pastor back on condition that he refrain from talking about race. The pastor could not accept this condition and asked to be appointed to another church. One church member wrote rather emotionally to the lay leader, "In the name of God, do something before it is too late. Get rid of this minister. Think of your community and the good churchgoer."

The pastor who elects to serve a church in a racially changing community does so at some personal sacrifice. This may include loss of income. One man was offered a choice of two churches. One was in a section which in a year or two would be changing racially. The other was located in a new and growing suburb. Furthermore, the salary at the suburban church was $500 per year higher than at the city church. The pastor, who decided to accept the church in the racially changing community, said, "I'm not sure that my superintendent should have left the decision to me."

In another congregation which was declining because of the changing neighborhood population, the pastor's salary was reduced because the congregation simply could not raise as much money as in previous years. When the denominational official offered to make up the deficit, the pastor replied, "No, the people are experiencing losses here and I should not accept outside support that is not available to them."

In still another instance a minister was sent from the position of assistant minister of a large suburban congregation to that of pastor in a racially changing neighborhood. The appointment came in the middle of the year. His predecessor, an older man, was anxious to get away at the first opportunity. At the time of the call the superintendent told the pastor that he was to "integrate the church" and warned him, "Your salary may go down."

Unfortunately this prediction proved to be correct. The first year the minister received a total salary of $5,500 plus $500 car expenses, plus the parsonage utilities. The next year the salary was reduced to $5,000 plus $500 car expenses, plus the parsonage utilities. The following year the salary remained at $5,000 plus $500 car expenses, but the pastor had to pay the parsonage utilities himself. Now, in the fourth year of racial change, the number of Negro members is increasing and replacing the white members who have moved away. The congregation has raised the salary by $265 per year, but the total remains well below what it was four years ago. The congregation has received no subsidy from the denomination.

The church situation in a racially changing community becomes particularly difficult when the pastor vacillates. We found instances of pastors appearing to have ambivalent feelings about making an effort to bring Negro members into the church. Some of these men felt that their colleagues in the ministry expected them to make an effort in this direction. So they talked about the necessity of developing an interracial fellowship without actually taking any steps toward this end. As a result the white laymen who wished to exclude Negroes became angry, and the pastors did not win any Negro members. Such pastors have sometimes been unjustly accused by their congregations of being integrationists.

In one congregation considerable controversy raged over whether or not to recruit Negro members. The general feeling was against taking this step although the pastor gave the impression of supporting such action. As a result the minister was severely criticized by his white members, largely without justification. In the church newsletter the pastor replied publicly to his critics:

Recently a man stood outside our church and declared to those who would listen that the present minister is going around knocking on doors and inviting Negroes to come to our church. This is an untruth, as is so much of the gossip we hear. . . . As a minister of Jesus Christ, and as the minister of this church, I shall strive to be a prophet of God's love for all mankind. However I am also a believer in democracy, and I shall be guided by the directives of our official board as I seek to minister in our community.

The Denominational Executive

An important, though somewhat behind-the-scenes, role is played by the denominational executive. His concern that the local churches under his jurisdiction serve all residents living in their communities is extremely important.

One of his important functions is setting the standards for the pastors. If the executive lets the pastors know that he expects them to attempt to lead their congregations to accept all persons living in the neighborhood, the pastors are more likely to work toward this goal.

There have been a few cases where the pastor integrated the congregation without the support of his superintendent. In a couple of instances the pastor brought Negroes into church membership despite some opposition on the part of his superintendent. However, the matter is sufficiently difficult so that few churches manage to accomplish it without the support and guidance of the denominational executive.

An important function of the denominational executive is the selection of the pastor. Frequently pastors are sent to particular churches to accomplish a certain task—such as to construct a building, to pay off a debt, or to integrate the congregation. The choice of the right man for the job falls largely on the superintendent. The success or failure of a church during a period of racial transition may depend on the skill with which the pastor is selected.

Equally important is the guidance the denominational executive can give to the local congregation. In a sense he is a kind of outsider who can see the particular church in a better perspective than can lay-men or even the pastor. He can also see the church in relationship to the other churches of the same and other denominations in the area.

The denominational administrator can be a source of support for the pastor and other local church leaders during the difficult time of transition. One pastor commented, "We were not sure how things would turn out. I always felt that the downtown office was ready to help us out if we needed it." It is important that a pastor feel that his superintendent understands the problems inherent in a racially changing community. The pastor's success cannot necessarily be measured by the easy criteria of an expanding membership and increased budget. Both of these items may decrease. The superintendent must understand what is happening in the community and in the church in order to be able to evaluate the work of the church and the pastor in true perspective.

Several pastors in racially changing communities whose congregations were still entirely white felt that they could take some action if they had more support from their superintendents. But while the superintendent can provide a degree of assistance, he cannot do the job for the pastor. In some instances lack of support appeared to be more an excuse than a reason for not recruiting Negro church members.

The attempt to recruit Negro members may result in resistance on the part of some laymen. The superintendent during such periods may receive telephone calls of protest from laymen. Some will demand the removal of the pastor. The superintendent must be prepared and stand strongly with the minister. Should the dissident laymen get the impression that the superintendent is wavering and considering replacing the pastor, the possibility of developing an inclusive congregation will be in grave jeopardy.

The White Laymen

The ultimate success of a church in a racially changing community depends on the laymen who catch the vision of service and respond to the challenge. They should clearly understand what the denomination is asking of them. It requests that they work toward winning the new residents of the neighborhood into the church. This will in the long term have the effect of bringing an end to the congregation as they have known it. They are asked to cast aside the comfortable aspects of the fellowship of which they have been a part, and view their church in the sense of a mission to the residents of the community. They are urged to overcome prejudices of long standing in their acceptance of the newcomers. They are expected to respond this way at a time when they may be under considerable pressure because of the transition taking place in the community.

In no church in this study did the majority favor receiving Negroes into the church in the beginning of the neighborhood change. During such a period many of the members are resentful of the Negroes moving into the community. They may not be able to prevent their moving into the neighborhood, but they do not have to welcome them into their church. Most of the white church members do not know Negroes as individuals, so it is easy for them to visualize the newcomers in terms of the traditional stereotypes.

A significant factor in considering the part played by laymen in the church frequently is their change of mind. In every church we found examples of persons who had been absolutely, and even violently, opposed to admitting Negroes into the church but who in the course of time experienced what amounted to a conversion on the subject. One pastor who is now in his fourth year in an inclusive church reported that all the members who in the early days were opposed to admitting Negro members, and who remained in the congregation, ultimately changed their minds. Some of the strongest adversaries became the most enthusiastic supporters. A pastor reported that a certain lady, the ex-president of the Woman's Society, has never spoken to a Negro in the church. Even she now admits that she is wrong but says, "I just cannot change."

In one congregation an elderly and highly respected member came up in support of the pastor who wanted to recruit Negroes. A number of other laymen who were wavering decided to support the pastor on the issue because of their respect for this

115

man. Similar persons were noted in several congregations. If a few members catch the vision, the probability of others coming along with them is greatly increased.

The laymen determine whether the Negroes are really welcome in the church. The pastor may persuade Negroes to attend the services, but only the lay members can make them a part of the fellowship. An incident related by a Negro member of an inclusive church in a northeastern city illustrates this point.

The Negro family purchased a home in the racially changing community because "it was a nice house." Their background had been Baptist, but they had not been particularly active in any church for several years. After getting settled in their new home they decided that the children should go to Sunday school. Inquiring of their neighbors they learned that Negro children were attending the predominately white Methodist congregation a block and a half up the street. The following Sunday they sent their two children to Sunday school.

The children were well received and enjoyed their experience. A day or two later the white minister came to call. He urged the parents to bring, not simply send, the children. After a week or two the husband and wife decided to attend the Sunday morning service. They found the people friendly and returned for several Sundays.

At the close of the worship service one Sunday

morning an elderly gentleman whom the couple had met several times stopped them on the way out of the sanctuary. He urged that they not only attend the church but become members. He told them how much the church had meant to him in his more than forty years as a member and said: "This should be your church. It can't survive unless folks like you become members. I hope that it will mean as much to you as it has meant to me."

The Negro couple discussed the invitation and came to the conclusion that they would join. The next Sunday when new members were received they were part of the group.

The Negro Laymen

Churches located in racially changing neighborhoods need to realize that Negroes must be persuaded just like white people to come to church. They do not stand outside white churches anxiously waiting for an invitation to enter. White congregations have struggled and agonized over the question of whether they should open the church to Negroes. When they have finally come to the decision to do so they have discovered that no Negroes came.

A white congregation should be aware of the fact that a Negro can select a church from a variety of all-Negro congregations ranging from large sophisticated ones to small store-front churches.

Furthermore the individual Negro is sometimes

reminded by the leaders of the all-Negro church trying to win his allegiance that he may not be welcome in the white congregation. He knows that in any predominately white congregation there may be at least some persons who will resent his coming. The chances of embarrassment are great if he attends a white church.

The Negro who is aware of the fact that some of the congregation may not want him may be overly sensitive. One Negro layman had been attending an inclusive neighborhood church for several years and was quite active. However, he had never become a member. Asked why he had not joined he replied that some members of the congregation did not really want him in the church. He continued to attend only because he thought the church school was good for his children. He could not—or would not—give any specific instance of when he had been made to feel unwelcome. He spoke of having made an announcement during a Sunday service at which he sensed that the congregation was resentful of his being there. Other Negro members of the same congregation did not express this sentiment.

Admittedly, the first Negro who comes to a previously all-white church may experience some embarrassment. White members need to be sensitive to the Negro's feelings. If the church is to develop an inclusive membership, there must be a first person. A white pastor once asked a Negro whom he had met in the community to come to his church. The man was not active in any church at the time. He asked the pastor if there were any other Negroes attending the church. When he got a negative reply he said, "I like you, Reverend, but I'm no pioneer."

The type of Negro who first joins is of great importance. In one congregation the first Negro member was a well-educated lady. Her home was described as a "showcase." She did much to dispel the conventional image in the minds of the white members.

In every church which successfully received Negro members, the white pastor had one Negro layman who helped to interpret the Negro to him. In one congregation the person who assisted him in this way was a college-trained Negro policewoman. She interpreted the Negro's feeling to the pastor and even assembled a list of books and articles for him to read.

In another church this function was performed by a Negro layman who was a government worker. The white pastor, a friendly and outgoing person, frequently used the expression "atta boy." One day his Negro friend took him aside and said, "Negroes, particularly those who were raised in the South, resent being called 'boy.' " The pastor understood the point and acted accordingly.

Some of the Negro members of inclusive churches have experienced conversions similar to that of the white members. In one such congregation a series of prayer and study groups was organized and led by the pastor. Members of both races participated in these small circles. The white members began to see Ne-

119

groes in a new and different perspective. Some of the Negro members also began to understand and deal with their anti-white feelings.

To Stay and Serve

In one sense every church which stays and serves the residents of a racially changing community is unique. However, in studying a number of such churches several common factors were noted. An awareness of them can be valuable to other churches which find themselves in a neighborhood in transition.

The churches which have stayed in a racially changing community have developed a concept of responsibility to the residents of their areas. Such congregations have a parish concept which leads them to look toward the persons who find the church convenient to their places of residence as a source of new members.

The contrasting viewpoint is a church which considers itself a group of people who gather together because of certain beliefs. It may consider itself a group called out of the larger society. A congregation of this type will not necessarily feel a special responsibility to the neighborhood in which the building is located. Unless a church has a sense of mission toward the inhabitants of the nearby community, it will continue to serve only white members, an increasing proportion of whom will be commuting back to the church.

The pastor has a strong voice in determining how the congregation will view its mission. If he devotes the major portion of his time and energy to cultivating his commuting members, he will have little available for seeking new persons from among the nearby residents. The church leaders, both lay and ministerial, must be aware of their responsibility to the residents of the neighborhood if the church is to continue in a changing community over a long-term future.

Churches which have survived in such communities have received and heeded early warnings of the impending community change and its implications for their congregations. One church had a rather dramatic indication of the future. A newspaper was doing a series of articles on communities around the city. As part of the feature a photographer was sent out one Sunday morning to take several pictures around the church. Shortly before the opening of Sunday school, the pastor showed the photographer around the building so that he could decide where he wanted to take the pictures. A classroom was selected because of its good lighting. The pastor went on to attend to other matters and the photographer proceeded to set up his equipment. The primary pupils arrived and the pictures were taken. That Sunday the first Negro children ever to attend the church school came. They happened to belong in the class that was being photographed. When the article appeared in the newspaper several days later, it was illustrated by a large picture of the class with the two Negro children present. Some of the laymen accused the pastor of planting the Negro pupils in the class, when in fact he had had nothing to do with their coming.

Most congregations learn of the impending change in a more prosaic manner. If the pastor is alert, he can do much to prepare his people for the transition. He certainly can make them aware of the probable course of events in the neighborhood. The denominational executive can be helpful at this point by meeting with local church leaders and helping them plan for the future in a realistic manner. If the church is to continue its ministry, it must take heed of early warnings.

The church which has successfully developed an inclusive membership has used its opportunities. An amusing incident led to the first Negro family joining a certain church. The pastor was telephoning persons who had moved into the general area of his church from a list supplied by the Welcome Wagon service. One call was answered by a lady who had recently secured a home some distance from the church. The pastor soon felt he had found prospective members. When he learned that the family belonged to a church of the same denomination in another city and that they were looking for a church in the community, he enthusiastically replied, "Look no more. We're your kind of people." At this point the lady on the other end of the line told him that they were

Negroes. The pastor, who might have been a little more hesitant in issuing an invitation to membership had he been making a personal call, did not back away. This Negro family was the first to join the previously all-white congregation. A church can never know when the opportunity may come—it had better be prepared to make use of it.

The matter of timing is important for the church which attempts to move from an all-Caucasian to an inclusive congregation. While situations differ there are times when crucial decisions must be made. The tendency is for churches to wait much too long before making an effort to win Negro members. The line of least resistance for the white congregation is to delay as long as there is a sufficient number of members to keep the church alive. If too long a period of time is allowed to elapse, the very survival of the church is endangered. Many prospective Negro members will have joined other congregations in the community. Furthermore, the white congregation which gets the reputation of excluding Negroes will have a difficult time changing its image.

The question sometimes arises whether it is possible for a congregation to move too rapidly in recruiting Negro members. The answer is that it is never too soon for a church to minister to persons who live in the community where it is located.

There have been instances of tactical errors in timing on the part of pastors. One minister, sensing that Negro people would be moving into the community, attempted to prepare his congregation to accept them into the church. At that time race was an impending but not an actual issue in the community. The result was that the pastor made the congregation angry over the matter of receiving Negro members at a time when there were no Negroes in the community to recruit. The neighborhood eventually changed, but much more slowly than anyone had anticipated. The attempt to force the issue in the abstract caused some of the members to make up their minds without having to react to real people. It is easier to be against a stereotype of "them" than to be opposed to individuals whom you can get to know.

During the period of transition a certain tension may arise within a congregation, first at the time when Negroes begin to attend services and again when they formally become members. After Negroes have become a part of the congregation, it may be some time before they are elected to positions of leadership. They are likely to become church school teachers before they are elected to membership on the finance commission or board of trustees. As the church begins to receive Negro members the church school tends to have large numbers of Negro children.

Some organizations within the church tend to resist admitting Negro members for a considerable period of time. This may not always be bad, however. The Couples Club in an inclusive church was composed of only white members. When asked about this, the pastor said that he did not object. He went on to say, "The white members need some group where they can discuss what they are doing in this church." The pastor had a good point. The white members were sharing an unusual experience; they needed an opportunity to consider and evaluate their feelings with one another.

One of the organizations which in a number of cases has resisted receiving Negro members is the Woman's Society. In no instance did the Woman's Society take the lead in receiving Negro members into the church or into its group. The women's circles in a church deliberately excluded the Negro pastor's wife. In another church, the president of the Woman's Society for two years refused to speak to any Negro although there were a number in the church membership.

For several possible reasons the Woman's Society tends to remain closed to Negroes. There is generally an age difference between the white women and the Negro women. The white women are usually older than the Negro women and consequently have different interests. The Woman's Society is usually one of the strongest groups in the church, as well as one with a range of functions and programs. The members have considerable contact with one another through a variety of meetings and activities. The group develops a strong fellowship and a feeling of self-sufficiency which may work against the easy acceptance of Negroes into membership.

There are certain courses of action which a church

in a neighborhood facing a transition had better avoid. No survey should be taken to determine whether the members favor or oppose Negroes attending the church. Several churches in this study did take such surveys. They ranged from a letter sponsored by a committee of the annual conference with a covering explanation signed by the lay leader of the church, to a telephone poll conducted by a woman on her own initiative. In every case the overwhelming majority of the members indicated that they were opposed to having Negroes attend or join the church. A survey can be harmful because it helps crystallize opposition to developing an inclusive congregation.

Churches should avoid passing resolutions concerning the admission or exclusion of Negroes. Most of the resolutions were not positive statements but said, "Anyone who comes to the church will be welcome, but no special effort will be made to win Negro members." The practical result of such action is to discourage any Negro who might be inclined to attend. Furthermore, people who commit themselves to a position publicly may later be reluctant to admit that they have made a mistake. Most of the churches which passed resolutions eventually retracted their actions.

Occasionally a congregation takes a positive stand in favor of ministering to all men. One such church, located in a border state, passed the following resolution: "The church believes that it should serve the community in which it is located by bringing the

Gospel of our Lord Jesus Christ to bear upon each person and family in the community, and . . . that this church which is a House of God, be open to the whole family of God, including the Negro."

This statement has not yet been tested.

Resolutions which exclude Negroes are harmful. Resolutions which welcome them are of doubtful value unless the congregation follows its statement of purpose with definite action. Obviously churches can take positive action without passing resolutions.

The congregation which stays and serves in a changing community needs to be sensitive to what is really happening in its neighborhood. Its leadership, both lay and ministerial, must be alert to take advantage of incidents which will bring people together and lead to an inclusive fellowship. The congregation must be willing to venture on a course that is unfamiliar to it. It must also be willing to risk the loss of the old and familiar for the new and unknown. Success is not assured, but this should not discourage any Christian group from making the effort. Churches which have ministered to all people have found it to be one of their most significant experiences. This sentiment was expressed by the lay leader of an inclusive congregation who said with obvious enthusiasm, "We've got a great church here."

VII

THE DENOMINATIONAL DILEMMA

That the Church should ever refuse access to worship or membership in its fellowship to any person because of race, color, or national origin is contrary to our fundamental Christian convictions. (From the Social Creed of The Methodist Church.)

The Methodist Church stands for equal rights of all racial, cultural, and religious groups. . . . We urge our pastors, upon whom rests the responsibility of receiving persons into the church to receive all who are qualified and who desire to be received without regard to race,

color, or national origin; and we individually and collectively pledge them our support as they do so. The
Methodist Church is an inclusive church. (From the
statement of the bishops of The Methodist Church,
Detroit, Michigan, November 13, 1963.)

The position of the denominations on the matter
of race is clear. Most Protestant groups have made a
strong affirmation of their belief that there is no
option for the local church but inclusiveness. The disparity between the statement of the ideal and the
actual performance on the local level is clearly evident. The action, or lack of action, of specific
churches is at times painful to behold. However,
before the church is cast aside as an organization
either unwilling or unable to live up to its ideals, two
factors should be considered.

First, the standards of performance which the
church sets for itself are not static. More is demanded
of the congregation in the area of inclusiveness today
than was required only a quarter of a century ago.
The section from the Methodist Social Creed and
the statement of the bishops quoted above are rather
clear in their expectation that the local church should
be inclusive. Interestingly enough, the Methodist
Social Creed of twenty-five years ago dealt largely
with social and economic issues not specifically related
to race. The issue of race was dealt with in two and a
half lines which stated, "We stand for the rights of
racial groups, and insist that the above social, eco-

nomic, and spiritual principles apply to all races alike." (From the 1940 *Discipline,* Paragraph 1712: 14.)

Second, the ideal which the denomination holds up for its local churches should always surpass the level of performance. The term "ideal" itself carries the connotation of an objective not yet attained. Indeed, the church is in peril when it reaches the point of being self-satisfied. Likewise the individual Christian who becomes satisfied with the depth of his spiritual life or his standard of conduct is the one most likely to be in the greatest danger of not seeing himself in true perspective. Institutions and individuals need to be striving toward perfection. The lack of perfection may be pardonable—the failure to strive is not.

Two Dilemmas

The first dilemma is the disparity between the denomination's statement of the ideal, carefully prepared by its theologians and duly passed by the appropriate legislative assembly, and the performance of the congregation whose members may or may not understand and accept the official position of their church. In no area of contemporary American life is this more evident than in the church located in the racially changing community.

A major problem facing the denomination is how to assist the congregation to move closer toward the ideal. How much pressure can a denomination exert upon its constituent churches without causing complete alienation and the withdrawal of members?

The second dilemma is the responsibility of ministering to two distinct groups which may be in conflict. The denomination is responsible to the white members who have been faithful over the years and who now need the ministry of their church in a time of upsetting social change. The denomination also has an evangelistic responsibility to the Negro people moving into the community.

Every community which is in the process of changing from a majority of white to a majority of Negro inhabitants has a number of white families who either cannot or will not move. Some of them will be church members. The church has a responsibility to these persons. Many have been a part of the congregation for a long period of time. They are numbered among the church's most faithful workers and supporters.

A Methodist pastor told of his parents who lived in a section of the city which had changed racially. Both were in their upper seventies. The house into which they had moved as newlyweds had been their home for over half a century. Now they were the only white family remaining in the block. Both were active in the nearby church which still had an all-white membership. The church was their only neighborhood contact.

The church is bound by loyalty to people caught in a system of population movement over which they as individuals have no control. This is the result of the church's concern for people. But the church has also a responsibility to the newcomer. The Negro moving into a previously all-white community brings his hopes and ambitions for himself and his family. He needs the ministry and guidance of the church as he seeks to become established in his new home, meet his friends, and raise his children.

Such a dilemma may result in a kind of stalemate. Decisive action would almost certainly hurt some of the faithful members. The minister is placed in a very difficult position. As pastor, his role is to comfort and aid his parishioners, not to override their feelings. The district superintendent may be in the same position for he has been and will again be a pastor.

The ideal would be an inclusive church in an interracial community. But the community continues to change. The congregation is not clear on what it wants to do or even can do. Thus, in a specific instance, the persons who must make the decisions may have to choose between what seems to be the lesser of two undesirable alternatives.

The Problem of Pressure

Given the official statement concerning the ideal of inclusiveness, what can the denomination do to persuade the local congregation to accept the position and act according to its tenets? It can take the time-honored way of education and persuasion. This is slow and may not work in every instance. What if the local congregation continues to reject the position set forth by the denomination? Should the denomination attempt to exert pressure on the local church? How can this be done?

The denomination can persuade a local congregation through its pastor. The denominational officials have considerable influence on a minister's career, while the lay members of a church are not subject to pressure.

The strategy of getting a local church to change its racial policy is usually begun by the appointment of a new pastor. A new minister is selected to go to a church with explicit instructions concerning what he should endeavor to accomplish. An example of this occurred at the time of a pastoral change in a community which then had about 25 percent Negro residents. The pastor was told by the superintendent that he was to receive Negro members into the church. At that time the congregation was all white. A meeting of the pastoral relations committee, the prospective pastor, and the superintendent took place one afternoon in the latter's office. At this meeting the superintendent publicly made his instructions clear to the pastor. The pastoral relations committee accepted the minister with the understanding that he was to attempt to win Negro members.

The same evening another meeting of the new minister and the pastoral relations committee was held at the church. The pastor wanted to see the church and parsonage, and to work out the details of moving. At this meeting a layman on the committee told the new pastor that the committee did not expect him to try to secure Negro members. He said the committee "had to tell the superintendent that we agree with his ideas on integration in order to get a minister, but we are not in favor of integration." The pastor's response was that he had been sent to the church to serve all persons in the community and would strive to do just that.

What happens if a church does not respond to the leadership of a pastor who has been sent to the church to accomplish a specific task? Can the denomination bring pressure on a local congregation to follow a policy that is contrary to the sentiments of the membership?

If the congregation is large enough to be self-supporting, the denomination cannot impose its will on the local church. A considerable degree of autonomy is prevalent in most Protestant churches, even in those belonging to denominations with an episcopal form of government. Most Protestant churches are inclined toward congregationalism, regardless of their denominational structure. The denomination simply does not have the power to impose sanctions on the local church.

From time to time the statement is made that local churches which do not follow the policy of the denomination in regard to inclusiveness should be expelled. In reality such an option does not exist for the Christian.

The Protestant tradition has emphasized freedom of choice. The individual has been told that he is responsible before God for his beliefs and actions. In practice he has the option of attending or not attending any church. If he is inclined to participate in a church, he may select any one of several with different types of programs and varied theological interpretations. Current ecumenical thinking has portrayed the denominations as coequal organizations.

The denomination cannot simply cast out the recalcitrant congregation. The church must always deal with those who fail to live up to its ideals. To cast out persons or groups neither helps them change nor cures the results of their actions. It only results in a feeling of self-righteousness on the part of those who remain on the inside and can compare themselves favorably with those excluded. Can the denomination expel a group for failure to follow a particular policy which happens to be much in the public view and fail to follow similar action where other violations are involved?

Reconciliation can take place only where there is communication. To simply expel those churches which do not adopt the denominational policy on integration would have made the existence of practically every inclusive church in this study impossible. The opportunities for interracial Christian fellowship which have been experienced by many of the members of these churches would not have been possible without the opportunity for growth. At one time or another every church which ultimately integrated clearly violated the standard of inclusiveness set forth by its denomination.

Denominational pressure was brought to bear on two churches included in this study. In the case of St. John Church described in chapter V the administrators effectively prevented the congregation from selling its building and merging with a church in the suburbs. The denomination had the power to veto the proposed sale simply by having the responsible officials withhold approval. In this instance the church had proposed to merge with an existing suburban congregation which did not particularly need the assets. One wonders what the decision might have been if the assets of members and finances were to have been used to start a church in a growing suburb where a new congregation was needed.

The decision on the part of the denominational officials to prevent the church's proposed move meant that the denomination had to take the responsibility for maintaining the church in its present location. There was not an immediate exodus of white members, but the attempt to win Negro members had to be subsidized. This was done by paying the salary of an assistant Negro pastor. When the continued decline in the number of white members resulted in the appointment of a Negro senior pastor, an even higher amount of subsidy from the denomination was required. If the denomination had not been prepared to support its demand with a considerable subsidy, it is probable that the church simply would have had to close for lack of sufficient people to maintain the building and pay the pastor. If a denomination insists on a specific course of action in a local community, it had better be prepared to provide an adequate subsidy to maintain the institution during the period of transition.

In another instance pressure was brought on a local church to receive two Negroes into membership. The couple attended and when they asked to join, they were referred to a nearby church of the same denomination which had an inclusive, although predominately Negro, congregation. A denominational executive learned of the incident and met with the local church board. In a reportedly stormy session the board was told that the Negroes were to be received into membership.

The result was the withdrawal of several families from the congregation. The day the Negro couple joined the church two white couples literally arose and walked out of the service. However, no large group of white members left the church as a result of this incident.

Approximately two years have elapsed since the Negro couple became members of the church. They regularly attend the worship service but do not participate in other church activities. Since the majority of members are older persons, there are few children. Only twenty children attend the church school. The Negro couple send their children to the nearby integrated church which has a large and thriving church school program. No additional Negroes have joined the church, although occasionally one attends a worship service. The number of Negro residents in this community has steadily increased during the past two years.

The pastor who came to the church since the two Negroes joined has been attempting to lead the congregation in facing its future realistically. Recently he took a poll of the members to determine what course they felt the church should take. The overwhelming response was to sell the property and relocate the congregation. Those who did not desire to sell at once preferred to continue as a white congregation as long as possible in their present location. Of the more than 50 percent of those who returned the questionnaire approximately five out of six indicated that they would not continue as members if the church were "actively integrated."

The present pastor reported that there is a great deal of resentment among the members because of the pressure exerted to admit the Negro couple. He indicated that he would not dare invite the executive to preach. One layman expressed the feelings of all of them: "To me there is not much any of us can do with the General Conference in power which will in the end decide for our churches. My only suggestion is to remain as long as we can."

The congregation did only what it was forced to do—it formally received two Negroes into membership. In the two following years it did not seek to win others. The result appears to be a resentful group which will hold out as long as there are enough persons to maintain the church. When they are unable to continue, the organization will collapse. There will be no nucleus of Negro members about which to develop the new congregation, because the white members are effectively keeping them out. When this point is reached the denomination will have to provide substantial subsidy while a new Negro congregation is being organized. If support from the denomination is not forthcoming, the church will be forced to close.

Regional Variation

The implementation of the general policy in a national denomination requires that regional variations be taken into consideration. While the gospel is not determined by the social and cultural context, its presentation is done within such a framework. Likewise the strategy for the local church will be greatly affected by the community in which it is located. In such matters differences in the various sections of the country become apparent.

In the North and West a vast majority of the Negro population is concentrated in the central cities of the metropolitan areas. While there has been some movement of Negroes to previously all-white suburbs, the overwhelming majority still live in contiguous Negro neighborhoods.

The speed with which the Negro community expands greatly affects a church in a changing community. When the increase in the Negro population in a particular city takes place slowly, the church may have time to get used to serving all people. Thus, the community which takes ten years to change from white to Negro may do so in much more orderly fashion than the one which completes the cycle in ten months. The latter may be one in which the blockbuster operates. Tension may run high. As the change comes quickly, there is practically no time for the members of both races to become acquainted individually.

In the large cities of the North and West the tendency to sell church buildings and relocate the white congregations has stopped in all but a few places. The generally accepted pattern is that of keeping the church in the community with the tacit understanding that the white members will eventually relocate their membership as individuals and not as a congregation. The building will not be sold. In due time a Negro pastor is appointed to serve a growing Negro membership.

The merger of the Negro jurisdiction into the geographic jurisdictions means that the same official has the responsibility for church strategy in serving both white and Negro people. It should result in better church coordination in all sections of the city. The merger also means that the departing white congregation cannot appease its conscience by having a convenient Negro Methodist organization to whom the building can be sold.

In the South the residential pattern of the Negroes living in the large cities appears to be following that of the North. The Negro community seems to be in the process of becoming a contiguous, geographically defined area. The continued pressure of the civil rights movement for school desegration may in the long term develop a consolidated Negro community which will result in the kind of de facto segregation—already prevalent in northern cities—of institutions organized along geographical lines. In one southern city a proposed urban renewal program had the effect of relocating the Negro population into a certain area. A new Negro school was under construction in a new Negro community. A variety of types of housing for Negroes was being erected. The result will probably be a new and better constructed Negro neighborhood more desirable than the old slum section, but a geographically segregated community nevertheless.

The idea of a Negro merely attending a white congregation is practically unthinkable in some sections of the country, not only to white persons but to the Negroes as well. In many areas, both North and South, very little communication takes place across racial lines between churchmen of the same denomination.

In sections where Negro and white churches are organized into separate organizations, it is common to find the white and Negro pastors, whose churches are only a short distance apart, unaware of each other's existence. In one city the ministers whose churches and parsonages were only three blocks apart did not know each other's name, although both had been at their respective churches for more than three years. In another instance two churches, one Negro and one white, were only 187 paces apart, yet one of the ministers was not even aware that the other church was of the same denomination.

In the South the idea of an inclusive congregation even during a period of transition is not considered an option. In practice the congregation relocates or, if this is not possible, the members simply leave and find a church in a white neighborhood. In some cases there is not even a remnant who come back to the old church and keep it open until a buyer is found. In one city a church building, larger and more adequate than many, was standing vacant and for sale, but no purchaser could be found.

What should be the course of the denomination in a racially changing community under such circumstances? Perhaps the best that can be hoped for is that the denomination will discover ways to conserve its property assets for the benefit of the incoming group. Coordination of the total denominational strategy has increased in some communities. If the

142

denomination is to keep its churches in racially changing communities for the residents who will be living there after the change has been completed, the administration will have to give more attention to overall and coordinated planning.

Some Bases for Decision

In every racially changing community some difficult decisions regarding local churches must be made. In many cases there may be no obviously "right" answers to the perplexing problem. In determining the course for a specific church there are several factors which can be useful in resolving the dilemma for the administrator.

What can be done to conserve the property assets of the churches located in communities which have completed their racial change?

The experience of being a part of an inclusive congregation has proved to be extremely significant in the lives of many pastors and laymen. This has been true even when an inclusive church lasted for only a limited period of time.

The denomination must never lose sight of the fact that it has a responsibility to minister to all residents of a racially changing community. It should endeavor to carry out this ministry through inclusive congregations and never let a failure prevent it from serving all persons.

Finally it must be realized that no neighborhood, even one which has completed a change from a white

143

to a Negro population, will necessarily remain static. Changes other than racial may take place in a community. The ministry of the local church must constantly be reevaluated so that it can present the gospel to whatever group may reside in its neighborhood.

VIII

THE FUTURE

The racially changing community is a phenomenon in American life which will continue for some time to come. The rate of change in the period ahead probably will be slower than in the decade past. Migration to the metropolitan centers was somewhat slower in the period of 1960-63 than it was in the decade of 1950-60.[1] Furthermore the Negro community in many cities is already very large. Because

---

[1] *Rate of Population Growth Slowing in U.S. Metropolitan Centers* (U.S. Department of Commerce, February 12, 1965).

of the size of its circumference there will be less outward pressure at any one point.

Once the racial change begins, the average urban neighborhood tends to complete the cycle from all white to all Negro. When this study was undertaken, the researchers hoped to discover communities which had become stabilized with an interracial population. None were found which met this ideal. With the exception of places where the presence of an institution, such as a university, provides a white housing market, all new residents who moved into a changing neighborhood were Negroes. An integrated community lasts only as long as the white residents who were there at the time of change remain. With no new white families moving in, the final result is predictable.

The number of Negro families financially able to purchase a house has increased considerably in the past decade.[2] This means an increasing number of Negroes will be seeking homes of their own. Racial restrictions have been and continue to be an important deterrent to their purchase of new houses. While some Negro families are securing homes in new subdivisions, the greater proportion seems to be moving into former white neighborhoods on the edge of the Negro community. It should be noted also that the expansion of a Negro community is no

[2] *Potential Housing Demand of Non-White Population in Selected Metropolitan Areas* (Housing and Home Finance Agency, Washington, D.C., April, 1963), p. 9.

longer confined to the central city. In some suburban areas, particularly the older suburbs, the small Negro section which has been in existence for a generation is now growing. The racially changing community is and will remain a problem in suburbia.

As the Negro population in the city expands, local churches and denominational officials will have to deal with the church in the racially changing community. The congregation cannot remain the same when white residents are leaving and Negro people moving into the neighborhood. Whether the people like it or not, whether they accept or resist the process, a "new" church will result. If the congregation elects to move, it will take along the name, the financial assets, and some members. As it begins its work in a new section, it will recruit members from the community in which it locates, persons who had no tie with the old neighborhood. In a short time it will be, for all practical purposes, a new congregation.

If the congregation decides to remain in the old community the result sooner or later—depending on the speed with which the neighborhood changes —will be a new group of members who have inherited the name and building of the former congregation. Churches usually operate that way—new members gradually are won to replace those who leave. The difference in this instance is the visible replacement of white members by Negro members. In an average church this process is continuous but at a much slower rate than in one in a racially changing community. The congregation which refuses to follow either course of action merely postpones the inevitable decision.

Self-support cannot be the primary goal for a church located in a racially changing community. The congregation may decline to the point where it can hardly keep the church open, much less carry on a vigorous program of evangelism. The denomination which takes a strong stand in the matter of race relations must support the congregation during periods of racial change. Assistance to the church is not only financial, although it most frequently takes the form of subsidy. It includes counsel on strategy and programming, and seeing that the right kind of pastor is appointed—one who can guide the congregation through the period of transition.

Every effort must be made to avoid creating dependency during the period when a church is receiving outside help. It is easy for a congregation to acquire a kind of missionary complex which will retard growth and self-sufficiency. The local group should be encouraged to carry the cost of its own program, maintain its building, and pay its pastor. Denominational assistance, where it has been most helpful without creating dependency, has gone into providing additional staff persons during the period of change or helping in a particular emergency such as the replacement of a furnace in the middle of winter.

The churches which have made the transition from white to Negro with the greatest success are those that have carried the major portion of the operating costs. Even in such cases the denomination would have come to the local church's aid if it had proved necessary. Perhaps more important than the actual cash contribution from missionary funds is the moral support the denomination can provide. Pastors and laymen who feel that their denomination senses the importance of the churches remaining and ministering to all people will conclude that their efforts are understood and appreciated.

The church which stays in the racially changing neighborhood and develops an interracial congregation passes through three distinct phases in relation to its community. When the congregation and the neighborhood both are composed of white persons, the church and its community have many values in common. The church lends ideological support to values which are held by the community in general. The pastor is the symbol of these values as he is called upon to offer the invocation and benediction at civic and community functions. The general community supports the churches. The presence of a civic official at a church function, such as the president of the suburban Board of Education being present at the consecration of a new church school building, is an example of the way community and church interlock.

But when the neighborhood begins to change

from white to Negro, there is a conflict of values between church and community. The residents of the community react in ways which are designed to preserve the neighborhood from the incoming Negro group. Associations are formed, pressure is put on the residents not to sell to Negroes. The church by its teaching of the equality of man before God and its emphasis on brotherhood may find itself in sharp conflict with the prevailing sentiments of the local inhabitants. This conflict may come into sharp focus in the official board of the church where some of the members wish to continue a "white only" policy while others want to admit all residents into church membership. The individual church member may here discover his ambivalent feelings. As a home-owner or businessman he may feel that it is to his advantage to exclude Negroes—as a Christian and church member he knows that he ought to work toward winning all men for Christ and his church.

The church which develops an inclusive fellowship must necessarily reject some of the community values. It must work toward goals which are the exact opposite of some toward which the community is striving, namely the exclusion of Negro residents. The inclusive congregation in an area of racial change becomes not only alienated from the original white community but also finds itself in conflict with the emerging Negro neighborhood. By trying to prevent the complete exodus of white residents it prevents at the same time the incoming of some Negroes. The congregation tends to become alienated from both elements in the community.

Pressure is brought on the members—both white and Negro—of an inclusive congregation in an area of racial transition to conform to the community standards. It is common for a person welcoming Negroes into a white church to be referred to as a "nigger lover." Similar epithets are given to some Negroes. Upon attending an integrated church they have been called "white lovers" by their neighbors.

A congregation which stays in a racially changing community and ministers to all residents despite opposition from the community is a church in mission. It develops a profound sense of purpose and unity. Its concern is to witness to all men, regardless of race or economic status, in spite of pressure brought upon it. Its members must not be hurt by slammed doors and unkind comments. Not all persons can take the pressure of community disapproval —some drop out. In one instance the members of a family disagreed over continued participation in a racially inclusive church. For two years the wife and daughter went to an all-white suburban congregation, while the husband out of conviction continued in the racially inclusive congregation. A high degree of spiritual discipline is needed to participate in such a church.

The members develop a profound sense of fellowship. Committee meetings take on an unusual significance. Members meet in one another's homes for meals and business. What is routine matter in other churches becomes an experience of deep significance for the integrated congregation.

As the neighborhood completes its change from white to Negro the congregation eventually loses its inclusiveness and becomes another all-Negro group in a Negro community. Many of those who had been a part of the church during the period of transition expressed disappointment that the sense of mission which they experienced at that time was ultimately lost.

When both the community and the neighborhood are Negro, the church tends to regain its harmony with the ideals of the community. These ideals may differ somewhat from what they were when the area had only white residents, but the relationship will be similar to that of the white church to its own community. The comment of a Negro pastor to his white colleague illustrates this point: "When you preach civil rights, you are being prophetic. When I preach responsibility, I am being prophetic."

The church starts as a white congregation which to a degree is in harmony with the ideals of its community. As the neighborhood changes the congregation develops a sense of mission if it sets in effect its true course and witnesses to a neighborhood whose ideals it cannot condone. When finally both the church and community are made up of Negro people, the church again shares many of the ideals of the general community. Its deep sense of mission is lost as it becomes a more "normal" church again.

The experiences of churches in racially changing communities may give some insight into the relationship of a church to the culture of which it is a part. When the culture accepts some of the same ideals of the church, the congregation can comfortably be a part of the culture. It may challenge the culture at certain points but there is a high degree of harmony. However, when the values of the culture conflict with those of the church, the congregation develops a sense of unity and mission. In communities of racial change this appears only during—not before or after —the period of transition. It exists when the values of the congregation are in conflict with those of the larger community. Does the congregation's sense of mission increase in direct proportion to its degree of alienation from its culture? Does the church's sense of mission decrease in direct proportion to its success in having its values accepted by the society?

In a study of an open housing covenant campaign in a small northern industrial city it was pointed out that many of the clergy looked upon the matter as a project "which could be quickly carried out and quickly forgotten."[3] The tendency of wanting to solve a problem as rapidly as possible and then forget about it is not only a characteristic of the clergy but of the total society.

[3] Henry Clark, *The Church and Residential Segregation* (New Haven: College and University Press, 1965), p. 203.

Racially changing communities are likely to be around for a long time. Such communities will continue to occur until the prejudice and discrimination against Negroes are materially reduced. In fact, there is some evidence that residential segregation in the large cities has been *increasing* in recent years.

The church in the racially changing community is not a problem which can be solved quickly or easily, because it is a series of problems in hundreds of cities and in thousands of churches. In each local situation the chasm caused by generations of segregation must be bridged over and over again. In every congregation there will be both successes and failures as the members attempt to respond to each other in terms of their understanding of the gospel.

This report has attempted to present what is actually happening in and to the churches located in neighborhoods of racial transition. There have been examples where the congregation has tried to live up to its ideals, and others where the church has acted in terms of its institutional self-interest.

An examination and reexamination of churches in racially changing communities can be a discouraging experience. Revisits reveal a continual drift from an integrated community and church toward a resegregated—that is, all-Negro—community and church. Evidences of real, lasting progress toward stable, racially inclusive churches and communities are few and far between. The local church in such communities is largely the "victim" of tremendous

154

social forces, rather than the "molder" of the social patterns. What is "success" in such a situation?

Success is a term which the church finds difficult to define. The easily measured institutional characteristics, such as membership size, growth, budget, and employed staff, have rightly been criticized. However, these criteria cannot be ignored entirely. A church is justifiably suspect if it fails to seek persons outside its fellowship even though it rationalizes its inaction on the basis of the spiritual perfection of its members.

Though the individual congregation may seem to be fighting—and losing—a rearguard action against overwhelming social pressures, it may be "successful." God does not call his people to be successful in the eyes of the world but to be obedient. It is the faith of the Christian that—in the long run—victory is with the Lord, and that his obedience will be vindicated. This kind of success is a possibility for the church in the racially changing community.

There are values to be gained in the present struggle. For the individual there is satisfaction and spiritual growth in overcoming fear, prejudice, and status considerations. For the congregation there is a spiritual vitality within a group dedicated to finding new patterns of Christian fellowship and common labor. These churches are some of the most alive and vital and exciting churches in the denomination. Great problems seem to demand and receive larger shares of dedication on the part of many ministers and laymen.

Each local congregation has the responsibility to minister in the name of Christ in whatever situation it finds itself. Every church—and particularly the church in a racially changing community—is responsible for its witness in the present time. It is in danger of failure if it allows the triumphs of a bygone era or the possibilities of some distant future to prevent it from ministering to the people who are its responsibility now.

The task will not be easy, as the Christian faith is not easy. Nevertheless, many congregations find themselves called to this service. Those which have responded to the challenge in the name of Christ have found grace sufficient for their needs—even in the racially changing community.

FOR FURTHER READING

Those who are intimately involved with racially changing neighborhoods will, of course, want to be familiar with the literature of the Negro protest movement, works by Martin Luther King, James Baldwin, and others. A scholarly analysis of this movement is "The Negro Protest," *Annals of the American Academy of Political and Social Sciences*, Vol. 357, January, 1965.

Sarah Patton Boyle, *For Human Beings Only*, New York: Seabury Press, 1964. To help understand the "other" race, one section interprets the racial feelings of Negroes to whites and another section interprets whites to Negroes.

E. Franklin Frazier, *The Negro Church in America*, New York: Schocken Books, 1963, and

Joseph R. Washington, Jr., *Black Religion: The Negro and Christianity in the United States*, Boston: Beacon Press, 1964.

These two studies of the Negro church in America help to understand the religious traditions among Negro people.

Group for the Advancement of Psychiatry, *Psychiatric Aspects of School Desegregation*, New York: Group for the Advancement of Psychiatry, 1957, and

Eleanor Leacock, Martin Deutsch, and Joshua A. Fishman, *Toward Integration in Suburban Housing*, New York: Anti-Defamation League of B'nai B'rith, 1965.

These two pamphlets deal with the psychodynamics of reactions of persons in interracial situations. In one case the participants were in the situation involuntarily as the schools were desegregated. In the other case the participants voluntarily joined community organization attempting to stabilize a changing community.

Luigi Laurenti, *Property Values and Race: Studies in Seven Cities,* Berkeley: University of California Press, 1960, and

Chester Rapkin and William G. Grisby, *The Demand for Housing in Racially Mixed Areas: A Study of the Nature of Neighborhood Change,* Berkeley: University of California Press, 1960.

What actually happens to property values in areas of racial transition? This question is studied factually in these two volumes.

Henry Clark, *The Church and Residential Desegregation: A Case Study of an Open Housing Covenant Campaign,* New Haven, Connecticut: College and University Press, 1964.

This is the story of the participation of the religious organizations in a campaign to get signatures on an "open housing covenant" in a small industrial city of the North.